HEAVEN'S MOVE TO SAVE AMERICA

THE GOD STORM

Published by Daniel Rubalcaba
ISBN 978-1-5480524-2-3 (trade paper)
Copyright © 2017 by Daniel Rubalcaba
DanielRubalcaba.com

Book cover design, and inside page layout
© 2017 by Nathan D. Fisher
IdeasAblaze.com

Scripture taken from the New King James Version. Copyright © 1982 by ThomasNelson, Inc. Used by permission. All rights reserved.

Printed in the United States of America
2017 – First Edition

TABLE OF CONTENTS

FOREWORD

I am honored that Daniel Rubalcaba would invite me to write the foreword to his book "The God Storm". My friend and colleague in ministry with the Assemblies of God Daniel Rubalcaba is a true bondservant of Jesus Christ! When you meet him and hear him, you know that his ministry does not follow current trends or common themes, but rather he is a man shut in with God, who has encountered God and speaks the heart of God. The reader of this book will encounter both God's zeal for His own glory, as well as God's heart for the people of United States of America. The God Storm based on Acts 27 reveals God's relentless love and determined purpose to redeem lost people! Anyone who has found him or herself broken heartedly praying for and interceding for a spiritual awakening in America, you must read this book! Any one who is grieving over the widespread spiritual and moral decay in our nation resulting in the public rejection of Biblical truth and our historical Judeo-Christian values, you must read this book! For anyone who senses that judgment is looming on the horizon and has cried out to God saying, "Lord, I have heard the report about You and I fear. O Lord revive Your work in the midst of the years, In the midst of the years make it known; In wrath remember mercy (Habakkuk 3:2)", you must read this book!

The "God Storm" is a sobering message revealing that God's perceived silence in the face of America's brazen sin, disobedience, lust, greed, idolatry, evil and iniquity, must not be misunderstood. Psalm 50:21 NASB says, "These things you have done and I kept silence; you thought that I was just like you; I will reprove you and state the case before your eyes." God is not like us, nor does He forget or wink at sin, nor does He overlook gross injustice, oppression, innocent bloodshed and arrogance. God will not remain silent, and when His word is ignored, He speaks loudly in ways that get our attention.

The "God Storm" is a hopeful message revealing God's determined purpose to have mercy on His people. The writer of Hebrews says, "God, after He spoke long ago to the fathers in the prophets in many portions and in many ways, in these last days has spoken to us in His Son, who He appointed heir of all things, through whom also He made the world (Hebrews 1:1,2)". Theologians say that God reveals Himself to us in two ways. God reveals Himself and speaks to us by general revelation, which includes His creation (Romans 1:18,19) (Psalm 19:1-4), and also via His transcendent intervention in human history. Job 38:1 says, "Then the Lord answered Job out of the whirlwind and said." God also reveals Himself and speaks to us by special revelation, which includes His spoken word (prophets), His written word (scriptures), and the incarnate Word (Jesus Christ). When people turn away from God's voice via special revelation (God's word), God often uses general revelation (creation, history) to speak to and drive His people back to His spoken word, His written word and ultimately His incarnate Word. Salvation can only be found when we turn whole heartedly and by faith to Jesus Christ! A good example of this happened on September 11, 2001. The Sunday after terrorists flew two commercial airplanes into the World Trade Center, church attendance around the U.S.A. was at an all time high. People who had ignored God for a long time were driven to seek God, and hear His word again. But sadly it was short lived awakening and within a matter of weeks, church attendance dropped to pre-9/11 numbers.

I first became acquainted with the ministry of Daniel Rubalcaba in 1996 when he visited the church I pastored in Cortez, Colorado. Our church had begun a season of prayer and pursuit of God seeking renewal and revival for our city and nation. We had scheduled him to preach both services on Sunday only, but after hearing him preach my spirit was deeply stirred by his words, and I knew his Christ centered message revealed the heart of God for His church and for America, like no one I had heard before. I asked him to please stay longer if it were possible, and he was only able to stay two more days. I immediately scheduled him to return as soon as possible. In 1997 Daniel again came to Cortez to preach a Sunday through Wednesday meeting, and once again his messages impacted our hearts deeply resulting in a deeper hunger for the presence of Christ! The Holy Spirit moved upon children, youth and adults who were stirred, broken and moved to much prayer at the altars seeking and pursuing Christ Himself! God began to do something special in our church and that four-day meeting turned into a two-week meeting. I once again scheduled Daniel in 1998 to come and preach a weeklong meeting. God continued to move in our hearts powerfully and the week- long meeting became an 18-month meeting where God visited our church with an awakening and revival that impacted children, many young people and whole families. That revival meeting impacted my family and my ministry profoundly. It was during this season of spiritual refreshing that I came to know the heart of Daniel Rubalcaba. He is a man of much prayer and fasting, whose pursuit of God is relentless. When I think of Daniel Rubalcaba, I think of the scripture that describes Jesus' earthly prayer life which says, "In the days of His flesh, He offered up both prayers and supplications with loud crying and tears to the One able to save Him from death, and He was heard because of His piety (Hebrews 5:7)". During that 18- month meeting I heard Daniel many days in the sanctuary crying out to God with loud crying and tears for the people of the United States of America and for our churches. The message of the "God Storm" was birthed out of those many seasons of prayer. I strongly recommend this book to you, as I know that it's message will be profoundly important to all of us in the coming days!

May God use this book mightily to usher in a new season of returning, repentance and revival in America!

– Dennis Rivera - District Superintendent of the Central District of the Assemblies of God.

PART 1

"He (Paul) said unto them, Sirs, I perceive that this voyage will be with much damage, not only to the lading and ship, but also of our lives. Never the less, the centurion believed the master and the owner of the ship, more than those things which were spoken by Paul...And when the south wind blew softly, supposing that they had obtained their purpose, loosing thence, they sailed close to Crete. But not long after there arose against it a tempestuous wind, called Euroclydon". (Acts 27:10-13, 14)

The key to successfully weathering any storm is solidity in Jesus Christ our Lord and Savior. The solidity we have in Christ, however, can only be defined by the severity of the storms we have encountered to this point. These obviously vary from person to person although there is one common denominator; we are all human. The storm I want to relate to in this book has its personal implications but is of a far greater dimension than any of us are able to fully understand. Because of our mental limitations, faith in God is an absolute prerequisite to our preparation for our tempestuous future.

The journey we have embarked upon contains us all, there are absolutely no exceptions. It doesn't matter who you are, what you own, what you know, or what your position might be; there are no exceptions. Denial will not excuse you from this journey; anyone who is convinced that they are not included in this journey has only succeeded in delaying their preparation for it. People of all religions, of no religions, and of every spiritual condition are included.

THE HOLY BIBLE

My platform of instruction and revelation is my own salvation through the shed blood of Jesus Christ. I have been "born again" according to the gospel of John 3:3. My source of absolute truth applying to every conceivable practical aspect of human life both temporal and subsequent eternal is the Holy Bible. The infallibility of The Bible is perceived only by those who are "born again"; it is scrutinized and open to debate by those who are not. I am not convinced of The Bible truth; I am born of it. The divine nature of The Bible provides supernatural equipping for those who are both children and ambassadors of it. This equipping provides divine ability for the communicating of the love of God both through word and deed. The empowered voice communicates the 'heart of God and is appreciated by those whose hearts are open though perhaps hated by those whose hearts are not.

EUROCLYDON

Euroclydon: a violent agitation; a south east wind raising mighty waves; a typhonic wind. A whirling unpredictable storm producing wind which blew in the Adriatic Gulf; definitely one to be avoided according to the apostle Paul; the destructive force of this wind was well documented.

Not the kind of wind any of us would like to get caught up in but…wait a minute; let's expand our thinking. Prophetically, this storm is not unique to any generation of people. It is present and relevant to all generations. It is the God Storm; the raging discontentment of God that has met many wicked societies in the past and is now an inevitable reality to ours.

PAUL'S WARNING

"Sirs I perceive that this voyage will be with much damage, not only to the lading and ship, but also of our lives".

Paul is completely aware of the lateness of the season and the danger that it represents at sea. More significantly, he has received a definite word from God removing any doubt that this journey will be tragic. Paul's warning goes unheeded because obviously these men know better. As emphatic as Paul was in his warning, the master and owner of the ship were more believable to the centurion in charge. Besides, Paul's recommendations were not convenient.

Now, a warning to this generation, to this lukewarm church;

STOP AND PREPARE YOU HEARTS for we are in the early stages of this ominous God Storm. In it there will be very much destruction and hurt. Return to God with humble hearts filled with brokenness and repentance. Return to the God of the Bible.

UNAVOIDABLE TRUTH

Paul simply could not convince these men of the peril that awaited them should they embark on this journey. Strong, determined, experienced seamen also (to a degree) aware of the danger but completely unwilling to listen to the voice of this 'religious man'. These sea faring men were foolish but they were not unintelligent; they were obviously skilled in their work. They could not receive Paul's word because they could not perceive his authority. Where there is not salvation there must be humility in order to hear God's voice; in them there was neither, therefore, they could not hear the warning of Paul.

This scenario has been repeated in our generation. Leaders and authorities in ALL positions of power and influence have been equally foolish. For a lack of humility, they have embarked on an incredibly dangerous journey and having arrogantly dismissed the warnings of God carrying with them a whole generation of people who have placed their trust in them.

Can we somehow avoid this ominous journey? NO. We are well into it already, as a matter of fact; we are far from the shore and feeling the effects of the tempest now.

SMOOTH SAILING BOYS

"And when the south wind blew softly, supposing that they had obtained their purpose, loosing thence, they sailed close by Crete".

These men had debated the decision to continue on; they know that there are dangers involved with decision they have made. It is obvious there are apprehensions present but after a period of time passes and with the winds being conducive and gentle, they begin to rest a bit easier thinking the decision has been a good one.

Devastating decisions have been made in our country for the last several decades. These decisions have defined our apostasy and have set us on a crash course with the God Storm. As time has passed, though, we as a nation have felt no divine repercussions as a result of our decisions and so have taken for granted they are good ones. Many have breathed a sigh of relief dismissing the warnings of the men of God as incorrect.

Imagine for a moment; the pioneering thinking of these wicked minds. "Abortion, hum, I think we're ok. Prayer removed from our schools, still no storm. All's well! The systematic brain washing of our children with the justifying of evil lifestyles, still no tempest. The removal of the Ten Commandments from schools and governmental buildings, and still the breezes blow favorably. Judges overruling righteous laws promoting their own social agendas, and yet the warm breeze carries us unabated. Immorality glorified, pornography mass produced, the traditional family being demeaned and redefined, and still no sign of tempest. Smooth sailing boys"!

Oh foreboding storm not far away; tempestuous wind of an

eternal source; blast from the nostrils of a discontented God. The God who is forgotten by many; misrepresented by others; taken for granted by multitudes, and dishonored by most. Yet, He is loved and served by a tiny remnant who like Paul have perceived the danger and are desperately seeking God for refuge, and for revival. Their voices of warning have gone unheeded; the journey has begun and they are prayerfully seeking God for direction even as the winds are increasing. Their cries go unheard in the halls of the elite and powerful. Among the hierarchy of educational leadership, they are dismissed as nothing more than inferior minds, poor out-dated and gullible souls; not a force but rather a farce.

CARELESSLY CAUTIOUS

"…they sailed close by Crete".

Sailing near a large land mass during a time of dangerous sailing had to be assuring and comforting, an alternative should winds become unmanageable. Stay just close enough; if not literally then at least emotionally anchored to its shores. Perhaps its shear mass can aid in shielding us from potentially damaging winds. "Keep the land within sight!"

This has become a way of life; an unspoken philosophy, a foundational concept upon which we are building all new religions from our new schools of thought. Love they say is the overriding issue and in so doing are justifying those actions God calls sin. Like the crew of the doomed ship who referred only to the distant outline of the massive island so do the religious philosophers of today; they refer only to the distant outline of God but horribly fail to commit themselves to him. As a result, this distant perspective of The Lord offers nothing more than a spiritual placebo and cannot protect the masses from their own self destructive paths. Keep God within sight! And in so doing we blindly press on toward a certain shipwreck. Oh people! To ask The Lord to remove the storm would be to ask that His nature be altered or to move the immovable; not hardly. It is not a matter of God's intervention but one of our navigation. God has given us many opportunities to adjust our spiritual course to no avail. Our trust must now be in His willingness and ability to bring us through the storm and safely back upon the shores of absolute truth and mercy.

PART 2

"But not long after there rose up against it a tempestuous wind called Euroclydon. And when the ship was caught and could not bear up into the wind we let her drive". (Acts 27:15, 16)

How quickly things changed; it seemed that in an instant the ship was being overwhelmed by the very wind they had supposed they had escaped! Turning the ship directly into the wind; they attempted to reach the shore. They were sailing near by Crete as a precaution for this very possibility and yet as near as they were to the land, even within sight, the strong winds made it impossible to reach. The seasoned sailors aboard had underestimated both the strength and suddenness of the Euroclydon just as so many others had before them. There was no way the ship was going to go where they wanted; at this point the storm was in control. A number of carefully calculated decisions had been made and yet the journey had become a desperate fight for survival itself.

TRUTH OR CONSEQUENCES

It could also be called the storm of consequence, indeed, as the consequence of not giving heed to the apostle's warnings. The Man of God's words seemed inconsequential, and although they didn't know it yet, the storm would ultimately destroy the ship.

What could possibly be the consequence of our national sins? It causes me to cringe and tremble when I carefully consider the question. I feel this way because of the nature of our sins. They reflect a cold indifference toward God. It isn't that the population doesn't believe that there is a God (statistics prove that) but that God is inconsequential. Neither is it that they hate God; in their estimation, He is simply not a factor in practical 'everyday life. "Perhaps God has an opinion of right and wrong" they say, "but certainly not an authority." Just as Paul had (from their perspective) an opinion but certainly not an authority! This being true of any society, makes it a breeding ground for sins of convenience which are ruthless, cold, and mechanical.

Woe unto cold hearts who would sacrifice the lives of the innocent for their own Godless conveniences! Woe unto a governing body that could blindly pass legislation in support of the wicked lifestyles of the people! Woe unto the church feasting in elegant parlors when they should be weeping between the porch and the altar! God of the tempest; have mercy.

Wouldn't it have been great if, according to plan, they could have pointed the ship toward the island, safely landing, and merely waiting out the storm season? That opportunity offered to them earlier through Paul, was now taken away by the sudden fierceness of the wind.

DRIVEN BY THE TEMPEST

Our country will go as far as the winds of consequence will blow it even unto the breaking apart of shipwreck and God will allow it if by that means He might advance His purpose and save the people.

How quickly things have changed in this new century; the fierce winds of consequence have risen incredibly; the masses have been stunned by recent occurrences. A devastating attack upon our own soil; leaving the nation reeling and haunted by the memory of the Twin Towers crumbling down onto the streets below. Hurricane Katrina viciously battering the Gulf Coast and leaving New Orleans destroyed; again the masses stunned by the shear dimension of the catastrophe. Unprecedented murderous violence within our schools causes the people to gasp in horror. The reactions of many to mostly everyday stresses and anxieties have intensified to monstrous proportions. Mass murders go unexplained having no comprehensible motives; obviously one of the most frightening forms of insanity. Politicians seemingly living in a totally different world, strangely aloof, bent on power, fame, recognition, money, and privilege. Our leadership is paralyzed and unable to make things better.

Cataclysmic occurrences and for a brief moment the nation pointed itself toward the shore of safety. The shore was God; the Creator we have kept just within sight, but it didn't take long to see, that the salvation of this nation would not come so conveniently. Unfortunately, we are a nation bent on continuing a journey of normality instead of repentance. "They have sown the wind, and they shall reap the whirlwind" (Hosea 8:7)

APOCALYPTIC MIND

The Lord had expressed His willingness to protect the ship and crew by conveying a warning through Paul. And even though Paul knew what the ships fate would be; he didn't have the liberty to leave it. He was bound to this journey and not because he had become a prisoner of Rome but instead a prisoner of Christ. Paul was the courier of God's purpose; The Man of God with the "message of life" to a lost world.

More and more, God is revealing His plan to a consecrated and praying remnant. They know as Paul knew and yet for them there is no release from the journey; they too are bound to the purpose of God being the messengers of The Gospel. This being true, how does the remnant prepare? First we must develop an apocalyptic mentality based upon the correlations between our society and historic ones which have been visited by the ferocious winds of God's Discontent. This coupled with intense and uninterrupted prayer will give us a prophetic perspective; It will deliver us from denial and create in us the proper mentality. A mentality founded on wisdom and rationale purified through the effectual fervent prayer of righteousness. It will not be one of gloom and doom but one of "responsible hope"…Ark Building if you would.

AVAILABLE TO GOD?

While the ship is being violently driven by the strong winds of consequence, it behooves us to turn the light of scrutiny upon ourselves. Imagine this whole scenario, viewed through the eyes of one totally uninvolved. Their conclusion would probably be as follows, "This is a desperately unfortunate ship, crew, and passengers caught up in a deadly storm; fighting with all their might to survive and yet, it doesn't seem probable that they will." Pretty cut and dried situation and it would have been, except for one thing or rather one person, the Apostle Paul.

As things progressively worsened, it became more apparent to the professional seaman that no human effort would save the ship and all those aboard from a watery end. The howling wind along with the waves crashing upon the ship must have been deafening while hopelessness increased; howbeit, unseen by the human eye was a glorious divine connection between Paul and God; and through this purely God initiated and God secured relationship, The Lord Himself was able to intervene and save the entire number from death at sea. (Obviously the Lord could have saved the ship. He could have calmed the storm but there are times when His purposes are better served by letting the storm rage.)

Our challenge is too visibly represent the invisible and audibly represent the inaudible; furthermore, it is too physically represent the spiritual. Being created and able to represent the divine is what is required. For most, the thought of being this, even approaching this, is inconceivable. This is viewed as the Mt. Everest of Christian desire yet, by most, understood as being personally inaccessible. But is it really?

WHAT HAPPENED TO YOU?!

Perhaps we need to start at the beginning. Paul, as you recall was the one who had so vigorously and violently opposed Jesus Christ represented in the early church although his understanding of it was different. He saw it as the necessary 'snuffing out' of a completely heretical movement and an affront to the true religion of Gods people Israel. He, being a man of conviction and also one in leadership, took it upon himself to lead the assault which would ultimately end this new scourge in the land. Well into his strategically planned operation, Paul was met by probably the least respected man in the list of Paul's 'least respected men!' *We all tend to make lists like that you know.*

"And as he journeyed, he came near Damascus: and suddenly there shined round about him a light from heaven: and he fell to the earth, and heard a voice saying unto him, Saul, Saul, why persecutest thou me? And he said unto him, who art thou Lord? And the Lord said, I am Jesus whom thou persecutest: it is hard for thee to kick against the pricks (stings). And he trembling and astonished said, Lord what wilt thou have me to do?" (Acts 9:3-6a)

This wasn't God's still small voice; this was God's stiff right hook and I assure you, Saul felt it. It wasn't the fall that hurt Saul it was the sudden stop that did it and lying on the ground, Saul was changed forever. We call this: 'high impact conversion'. This was God dealing with the rebellion of the man; the stings of conviction hadn't stopped Saul but the right hook of God's correction knocked the man from his pride onto God's purpose.

These days we have softened the blow; we have pandered to the sinner in politically correct terms and methods and it is not the Spirit of God but rather the flesh. We have padded the pews, the floors, the sermons, and even the consequences just in case God knocks someone down again. We don't want to seem too radical you know. We want folks to come back next Sunday. God was able to use Paul (the converted Saul) during impossible conditions because he started out right; i.e. flat on his back and overwhelmed by the awesome God he had thought he was serving all along. That's what happened to Saul. What happened to YOU?!

PART 3

" **A**nd running under a certain island which is called Clauda, we had much work to come by the boat. Which when they had taken up, they used helps, undergirding the ship; and, fearing lest they should fall into the quicksand, strake sail, and were driven." (Acts 27:16&17)

PROPHETIC REASONING

To prophetically place the U.S.A. into this 'ship wrecked' scenario is far more accurate and realistic than most people would like to believe, as matter of fact, most would probably consider it ridiculous or even anti-American. Considering the fact that the Bible itself has become anti-American in many sectors of our society;

no attitude would surprise me at this point. History has proven that being incredibly dogmatic about any issue does not guarantee that the person is right about that issue. This is especially true when we are attempting to inject prophetic reasoning into a society where the humanistic and sensual perspective is hugely dominant. Inaccuracies occur when we prophecy out of our own hearts i.e. when we are too personally involved in the situation; our minds being what they are, take intense emotions and make them speak for God; the end result is inaccuracy and disqualification. Being aloof, detached, or uninformed is not the answer either; being separated unto God is the answer and is the fail-safe. The less attached we are to this world the more able we are to speak prophetically into it. God will be glorified in every society; our hope is that in ours it will be through revival; it could very well be through painful judgment. Either way, the 'prophetic heart' works to keep the people informed of the process. People of faith need current information (prophetic information) for their prayer lives and for their decision making process.

THE LIFEBOAT

Frigid temperatures, driving snow, freezing rain, all contributed to the increasing desperation of the men. Driven dangerously close to a small island, every effort was made to avoid running against its shores. Then seeing that the lifeboat (which was in tow) was also in danger of being destroyed or lost was with great difficulty taken a board. Though the boat was cared for as a possible means of escape, it would be made perfectly clear that the only escape for all of them would be in surrender to the prophetic directions of Paul.

As our nation is driven farther and farther into waters of desperation, it will be more apparent that only a miracle from God will deliver us from our stubborn refusal to heed His warnings. We have taken great care and precaution to have in place systems of security or escape in times of national emergency, and yet, history's greatest military will not save us nor will her greatest health care system nor will her greatest economy nor will her greatest educational system. No. Not even the greatest rescue organizations the world has ever seen will be able to save us. Hope lies within those few who love Christ more than words can possibly say; those who were in the beginning overwhelmed by Jesus and have been ever since. Hope lies within those few, who like Paul, have said with complete brokenness and surrender, "Lord what would you have me to do."(Acts 9:6) Hope lies in the beating heart of Jesus embedded within the corporate breast of believers called 'the remnant of God'.

REPENTANCE NOT ADJUSTMENTS

The power of the storm that batters and drives this ill fated ship cannot be overstated. Likewise, the consequences we face as a nation are huge and cannot possibly be exaggerated. We find these seasoned mariners dodging islands and sand bars like a slalom course; making desperate course changes to avoid certain shipwreck. Likewise desperate attempts to "educate ourselves out of trouble" have not curtailed our social woes. Teen pregnancies…educate! Sexually transmitted diseases…educate! Drug addictions…educate! AIDS…

educate! Inner-city violence…educate! The problem with this is that the 'educators' do not have concrete answers. What they offer at best are slalom type adjustments which cannot turn the ship around; they can only delay the inevitable. Repentance is the answer but unfortunately it is an option the nation is still unwilling to consider, and so, the storm rages on.

BRACING

"Tighten up the ship"! "Cast forth the helps"! Because of the relentless beating the ship's hull was receiving, heavy cable like ropes were wrapped completely around the vessel then tightened in hopes of strengthening the hull.

Have you noticed how desperate our efforts have become to tighten up our ship? 'Increased Security' has almost become our new motto. "Increased security is necessary within our nation and now at our nation's boarders", they say. Why? Because we have enemies who must be kept out? No my friend. Our perceived enemies are really only opportunists who are seeking access in order to consume the remains left behind by an enemy which is destroying our nation from within…'rampant sin'! We are imploding due to the immense vacuum created by the nation's rejection of God and its systematic repudiation of its Judeo-Christian roots.

TINY MINDS

Clauda is a small island with rugged and dangerous shores. Slowly and carefully approached, Clauda could be considered a temporary refuge if absolutely necessary but certainly not during a violent storm like this one. It was actually safer to make the required maneuvers in order to miss the island entirely. In this deadly storm, the island represented much more peril than peace; realizing this, the crew chose instead the open sea.

Caught in the bowels of this God Storm, when everything is at stake, we cannot seek refuge in the tiny minds of tiny men. Now I want to dispel the idea that I am being sarcastic at this point. First of all, I am not referring to the hearts of men but to the minds of men, the literal thinking, thought processing, conclusion drawing part of man. When I refer to theirs as being tiny minds, I am not comparing their minds with mine, as a matter of fact; they are much brighter than I am in most aspects. These are the most respected social problem solvers of our day; therefore, I am not comparing their mental capability with ours but rather to the sheer, incomprehensible dimension and complexity of this storm. We are in the midst of a God Storm; driven by the powerful and dangerous gales of His Discontent; any attempt to humanly 'figure' our way out of it is completely ridiculous. That's why we (like the mariners) are far better off to steer clear of all those who think they have answers; they are at this point more dangerous than they are helpful. We don't need more educated guessers. What we do need are men and women of God like Paul, whose relationship with God was so rich and intimate and whose life was so valuable based upon God's purpose that He was willing for the sake of one to save the sum. Hallelujah!

USABILITY

For the sake of deeper understanding, let's remain within the realm of general Christianity and examine what defines personal usability under the simplest criterion.

For example; Wonderful deeds, Exceptional deeds, Admirable deeds, Ordinary deeds, Acceptable deeds, Tolerable deeds, Intolerable deeds. Obviously (according to these categories) the usability of an individual will be determined by the standards established by or adhered to by those who will ultimately decide. What is considered Admirable by one group may not be by another, therefore, the individual may be usable in one but not in the other. What is completely intolerable in one may not be in another. The point is, to be usable in a church, church organization, Christian organization, Christian group, Para-church group, or any human run church org. is one matter; but to be usable to God is a whole other issue. The usability determined by God (also a wonderful form of God's favor) is what current conditions demand, indeed, the kind of person that God can use to rescue 'whole nations' in a day. How big was Paul's relationship with God? It was big enough to be heard above the thunderous sounds of Euroclydon. How big is your relationship with God?

PART 4

" And we being exceedingly tossed with a tempest, the next day they lightened the ship; and the third day we cast out with our own hands the tackling of the ship. And when neither sun nor stars in many days appeared, and no small tempest lay on us, all hope that we should be saved was taken away." (Acts 27:18-20)

STORM AWARENESS

For many years, the Lord has shown me an approaching storm. He has kept it at the forefront of my mind, a perpetual and inescapable reality, not foreboding nor nerve-wracking yet as real as God has been.

It wasn't long after the Lord had saved me that I began to feel a powerful call to prayer. Along with the inexplicable joys and sensations of salvation, I received a sudden and overwhelming awareness of God's heart. It was an emotional awareness that was communicated through my own heart and a consciousness I hadn't known nor possessed before. My life brimmed with desire to serve God; I was filled with burning purpose but lacked direction so I began to pray. I emptied a closet, threw in a bean bag, sealed the door to any exterior light, closed it, and prayed (for hours at a time in complete darkness). It was there that the Lord began to teach me about a storm, a storm that would bear the characteristics of God Himself, thus, The God Storm. It is impossible for me to think of it in an impersonal way. I strongly pray that it will be the same for you, the reader.

TAKING ON WATER

The intensity of the tempest hasn't abated at all. The wind drives the ship while the waves continue to punish the hull. It is at this point that the crew begins to lighten the vessel. It is very possible the decision was made to lesson the burden on the hull as a precaution just as employing the "helps" was earlier. Every precaution was taken to prevent the ship from taking on water. The decision to cast off the very tackling of the ship, however, would strongly indicate that the ship was already 'taking on water'. "Lighten the ship. Bail the water!" These are last ditch efforts to keep the vessel afloat.

Why do we suddenly have so many corporate mergers? Why are so many of our corporations being sold to foreigners? Why are there so may federally funded corporate bail outs? Why is there such a 'money grab' using shady finance tactics? Why do credit card companies get away with 'stuff' you and I would never be allowed to do. Why has the stock market become so unstable? Why does the stock market rise and fall according to the emotions of investors and as a result has been mostly artificially stimulated to create a perceived strength? These are last ditch efforts to keep the vessel afloat. Why?! The ship is taking on water! The vessel is sinking. Oh how devastating are the winds of consequence, the storm of God's discontent. Decadence, air of invincibility, and national denial has set us up for a colossal surprise.

ONE MOMENT THERE AND THE NEXT GONE

What do we do now? Well, we do what the seamen did; we must lighten the ship. The crew's decision to lighten the ship didn't save the vessel but it did put them in a place where God could save them from a watery grave. Had they not lightened the ship, it would most likely have sunk in the midst of the sea far from the island where they were eventually saved. I have seen a couple videos taken of sinking ships; both were very large vessels and both sank rather quickly. It is an astonishing and eerie thing to see; such a huge vessel and it just seems to disappear; one moment there and the next it is completely gone, as though it had never existed. It wasn't God's will for the vessel Paul was aboard to utterly disappear at sea. The vessel was precious but not of itself; it was precious because of its human cargo, chiefly Paul who was the courier of God's word to the nations.

Our 'great nation' became great because it has been the world's chief courier of The Gospel. Like Paul's vessel, this nation is great but not of itself; it is great because of the Gospel it has cherished and carried to the nations. Though it is now perilously driven by the Winds of Consequence, it is not God's will for it to sink into oblivion, disappearing as though it had never existed. I repeat, it is not God's will but it is not beyond the realm of possibility.

*Note these scriptures, "How much has she glorified herself, and lived deliciously, so much torment and sorrow give her: for she saith in her heart, I sit a queen, and am no widow, and shall see no sorrow. Therefore shall her plagues come in one day, death, and mourning, and famine; and she shall be utterly burned with fire: for strong is the Lord God who judgeth her. (Rev.18:7-8)

*Again take note of how quickly this calamity will take place: "...for in one hour is thy judgment come; ...for in one hour is such great riches come to nought...for in one hour is she made desolate." (Rev.18:10; 17; 19)

Obviously this is speaking prophetically of 'that great city Babylon'; it is futuristic in nature. I am not saying that this particular city represents the United States neither am I saying that it does not. What I am saying (with great conviction) is that this is a literal occurrence and will literally come to pass. If I were a betting man, I would not wager money that 'this city' does not somehow relate to us; much less would I wager my life and the lives of my family! Would you? For us to avoid this dreadful possibility, we must lighten the ship.

TOO HEAVY

When the decision was made to lighten the ship an evaluation of priority was made. Amenities were cast away the second day and on the third day the tackling was committed to the sea bottom. All that remained on the ship were the things that were absolutely necessary. The ferocious power of the storm made it easy to let go of these things, many of them very valuable.

Jesus said," No servant can serve two masters: for either he will hate the one and love the other, or else he will hold to one, and despise the other. You cannot serve God and mammon (money). And the Pharisees, also who were covetous (loved money), derided (scoffed at) him. (Luke 16:13&14) "For the love of money is the root of all evil..." (1Tim.6:10) Jesus and the apostle Paul spoke absolute truth and yet the Pharisees mocked. Why? First of all, to love money is an incredible evil because out of it (like a root) grow all other evils. The Pharisees mocked because they bore within their hearts this evil. Secondly, because they were not confronted with their mortality at that moment; they did not fear for their lives, therefore, they could not be forced to re-evaluate their priorities. It is this very sin that we must throw over board. From this root has grown a huge society strangling mind set. This covetous monster with its money loving tentacles must be thrown over board if we are to have any chance of survival. What will people do for money?! Look closely at our society; therein lies the answer. "Lighten the ship"! Better stated," Lord forgive our sins! Forgive our love of money."

NAVIGATIONAL OPTIONS

The density and relentlessness of the storm is amazing and well characterizes the fearful determination of God when He has been pushed too far. They hadn't seen the sun or the stars for days; these being totally shrouded by the storm denied the sailors their own location and all navigational options. Knowing that within this area lay the dreaded Syrtis Sands where upon countless ships had wrecked, caused them to lose all hope of being saved.

This horrific Euroclydon was a foregone conclusion; nothing could have prevented this storm; it was going to blow and churn like crazy regardless of who was sailing upon the waters in its path. It was and is today respecter of neither man nor beast. But remember, it was and continues to be predictable.

There is no navigation in this storm; actually it represents the end of navigation. It represents the commitment to something which is an absolute conclusion. For instance, the murder of a child, once committed how do you re-navigate it? Can it be undone? Will there be consequences for the one who did it? (For the crew of Paul's ship, the final navigational option given them was, "Stop; stay". After that the Storm of Consequence enveloped them.) How about when 50,000,000 babies have been murdered (legalized abortion)? How do you re-navigate that? Can it be undone? Will there be consequences for those who did it and for those who approved? Indeed, the last navigational option given was, "Thou salt not kill...whoso shall offend one of these little ones ...it would be better for him that a millstone were hanged

about his neck and that he were drowned in the depth of the sea."
(Ex. 20:13; Matt. 18:6)

HOPE

Although the crew and the others had lost hope, there was hope howbeit unrealized. God was in the storm and had a plan for the salvation of all. Paul was about to reveal unto them the God who would save them; but before that, he would establish his authority in Christ by saying, "You should have listened to me......!."

PART 5

"But after long abstinence Paul stood forth in the midst of them, and said, sirs you should have harkened unto me, and not have loosed from Crete, and to have gained this harm and loss." (Acts 27:21)

ABSTINENCE

The men were depleted of energy but they wouldn't eat. I doubt they had slept either. From the moment they were engulfed by the storm, it's been a struggle for survival itself. Every thought, every second, every effort spent on life; the struggle to retain it and to somehow survive this monster storm. Not even the most basic of human necessities were taken into consideration. No time, no desire, no hunger. Our priority is to survive. Who can think of food at a time like this? Indeed, much less the dainties of life, the extravagance of abundance, or the unbridled trespass of sin. What neither man nor beast could pry from these strong armed men, the tempest has removed even from their minds.

God have mercy. The multitudes in our land will not reach out for life until they are convinced they are losing it. We Americans are willing to fight for our rights; our constitutional rights. We will also fight for our rights to alter the constitution in order to better facilitate our sin. We will have our rights and we will not have 'good and bad' defined by a bunch of radical fanatical Christians! We are an educated people. We are not bound by ideology. We will delight in every lust and desire. We will with-hold nothing from our enjoyment. We are Americans come hell or high water."

Understood! But, answer this. What about the God Storm? What of Euroclydon that roars incessantly. How will our nation bear up into its supernatural waves? I tell you, that as this apocalyptic storm increases, the flamboyant and audacious sinfulness that defines this generation will suddenly be forgotten. My heart weeps over the prophetic truth that grips my soul. The unthinkable now seems unavoidable. Abstinence will rule the hour when finally the people are ready to hear the Voice of God.

PEACE IN THE STORM

Relentlessly the storm continues to pound the wounded ship and the devastated spirits of all those aboard. Having lost all hope of ever being saved, the men woefully await the moment each will encounter the frigid waters of the sea. Slapped and tossed about like a mouse taken by a cat, each seaman is completely subdued and broken, powerless to make even one more attempt to escape the unavoidable jaws of the tempest. Cold and dizzied by the whirling clouds and blackened skies, an incredible light begins to shine within their hearts. Reminiscent of Jesus walking upon the water, Paul approaches them standing upon a promise. Leaning into the wind, staggering first to the left then to the right Paul begins to shout above the howling storm. "You should have listened to me and not have loosed from Crete"!

As the God Storm grinds on, hopelessness will ultimately envelope the people of our land. Many will have lightened their lives of burdensome sin while others have rearranged priorities after sincere soul searching. Churches will begin to fill again with serious seekers and repentant hearts; no longer will the damnable heresies of 'lukewarm Christianity' litter the decks of the ship. All of these actions will serve an important purpose but it will not be apparent to the people immediately, for the storm will rage on for a while longer and as it does, they will continue to despair more and more for their lives. It will be at this point in our country's history when the 'remnant of God' and 'the soul winners of the Lord' will be seen by unveiled eyes. They will have a perfect 'peace in the midst of the storm'. This peace will define them and distinguish them from all others. Not at all disoriented by the storm, they characterize solidity and authority, indeed, the heart and soul of a new leadership.

HARM AND LOSS

Paul expresses the contents of his heart; he begins by telling them of the significant loss they've experienced as a consequence of not heeding his warnings; he speaks of both human injury and chattel losses. Paul wants this fact to be completely understood before he goes on to reveal the promise of God's salvation. Salvation must wait until the consequences of sin can be effectively preached but that won't happen until the people are humbled, oddly enough, by the very same consequences.

During the first part of this tempest the seamen made desperate efforts to survive its sudden fury. Now all efforts have ceased. The storm has won. Any hope they experience now will not come as a result of effective navigation or of the storm's subsiding. Instead it will come from their faith in the promise Paul delivers from The Lord. Had they had such faith at Crete they would have never left the Fair Haven.

THE WHIRLWIND

While driving through Las Vegas Nevada some months ago, I noticed a couple of advertisement billboards representing a dark and lucrative aspect of their entertainment industry. They were boasting of having had "invented new sins". The flamboyant nature of this wickedness is frightening. (Incidentally, I know a special brother in Christ whose 19 year old son was recently murdered on the streets of Las Vegas.) Sin City? Listen folks, only a desperately fallen nation can 'birth and sustain' a Sin City.

"With the whirlwind, I will visit this nation. I will purge and purify it. In the whirlwind I will go about the land and declare my goodness, mercy, and righteousness." This the Lord prophetically spoke to me while preaching in a small town in Wyoming.

The whirlwinds I have experienced from my boyhood in Colorado were small and delightful; the ones the Lord showed me here were neither. It was 14 years ago when the Lord unfurled these prophetic words to me. As the Lord spoke these words, I also experienced a vision. In it, I watched a tornado moving slowly across the landscape of our nation. *God would begin to visit the nation with devastating tornados and hurricanes and they would come with increasing frequency and intensity. Initially, they would be limited to rural areas but eventually would begin to visit the more populated areas and cities. They would increase even into the winter months. In 1997, The Lord showed me a storm as a lion crouched in the Gulf of Mexico prepared to pounce upon the land. Katrina? (How accurate these revelations have been and will continue to be, until the people are prepared to once again hear the Word of the Lord.) 'The Whirlwind' represents one more aspect of the Euroclydon. Obviously these storms have caused much 'harm and loss' yet I am convinced that these are only the early stages of this apocalyptic journey.

NOT READY YET

I remember watching in horror as the second airliner flew into the tower. I felt dazed by the whole calamity and I know I wasn't alone. We gasped together. We cried together; and we still mourn together. I wasn't surprised though; The Lord had spoken prophetically in 1997 saying that His purging of our nation would begin in "… your nation's capitol and in your greater cities." The Lord had also said to me that I should "…prepare my heart for astonishment". He assured me that it would be with purpose and that I should be prepared emotionally so as to not be overwhelmed by the power and dimension of the things He would allow or bring about. He also said that He would bring an invading army but that none of us would know when or how they arrived. No, I wasn't surprised when I heard what was happening in New York City.

What was powerfully revealing to me was what took place soon after the terrorist attacks. A few well known ministers of the Gospel were given an opportunity to comment on what had transpired, and this, before a national television audience. All spoke in common of the love of God and how that He was with the suffering and mourning. Both true statements. Many other very warm and comforting things were said of The Lord, things I know I would have appreciated had I or one of my family members been a victim. All the pain and destruction was attributed unto the devil and his evil devices. The Lord on the other hand was completely dismissed of all involvement; He had absolutely nothing to do with what had taken place. The devil in these evil terrorists was the culprit!

There were a couple of exceptions though. These ministers began to speak of the holiness of God and the consequences of sin. Perhaps these attacks had something to do with the evil character our society has taken on. Perhaps God was at last holding Americans accountable for the sins which have become common and acceptable. There was an immediate uproar! How dare these Bible thumpers even suggest that we good citizens had anything at all to do with what these evil terrorists had done! These preachers are un-American! Send them to Afghanistan!

Do you see? The seamen aboard the ship were ready to hear the words of Paul. The consequences of their decision had convinced them and they were ready. America is not ready yet and so the God Storm will continue to rage on.

HEAR NO EVIL, SEE NO EVIL, SPEAK NO EVIL

For over 2 decades, I have traveled from state to state and from city to city preaching the Gospel to whomever will open their doors to our ministry. Each church has its own personality whether big or small, rich or poor. Definition, however, in many churches has become important and efforts are carefully made in order to define the church in a certain way. Size, location, prosperity, political influence, education, worship, spirituality and so on are ways churches are defined. Unfortunately, most churches have lost sight of what really defines the true church.

The church is supposed to represent the divine perspective, the eternal God. The perspective of God defines the American church by the condition of the society it preaches to. It is a nation built upon the foundations of God's Word. Her purpose has always been a missionary one. It is an heritage. If this passion is alive and vibrant, we are called to maintain it. If past Church leaders have lost this passion, we are called to regain it. When things are in divine order, the Gospel is America's greatest export. This is what defines the American church.

The church, however, has turned inward. It has become more concerned with its own success. Its heroes are contemporary ones not necessarily historic ones; they are the architects and builders of the most successful, most influential, fastest growing churches in America. Astonishingly enough, there is now a list of the 'who's who' among American churches. Confronting the society's sins is obviously counter-productive. "We are not here to make the people feel worse than they already do." They say, "We choose compassion over conviction." Their policy is: Hear no evil, see no evil, speak no evil and from a human perspective, they are incredibly successful. (Once again there are wonderful exceptions to this mentality also.) Realistically though, the majority of those 'most visible and most famous' seem detached from the current peril and from the prophetic warnings of God. This part of American Christianity cannot represent the Peace of God in the midst of the storm. Why? Because, they are either denying the storm or they are ignoring it.

PART 6

"And now I exhort you to be of good cheer: for there shall be no loss of any man's life among you, but of the ship. For there stood by me this night the angel of God, whose I am, and whom I serve, saying, fear not, Paul; thou must be brought before Caesar: and, lo, God hath given thee all them that sail with thee." (Acts 27:22-24)

IN THE WIND

The Apostle Paul was no stranger to trials and tribulations. He is not surprised by the situation he finds himself in now. I wonder what the Apostle's prayers were during those terrible days. Was he sure he would survive? It's apparent from Acts 27:10 that Paul believed his own personal welfare would be endangered during this ill-advised journey. He knew he was on a mission but would this ferocious storm change everything?

This was my most difficult discovery after launching out on full time itinerate ministry, the storms along the path of God's will. They've deeply tested my faith and resolve through the years. There were times when my ministerial life was in survival mode. I wasn't sure what the outcome of my efforts would be. Consequently, I gradually redefined success and certainly not because I had huge successes or multitudes of them. Experience has taught me not to attach my hope to ministerial outcomes. It's the rubble left behind by unexpected storms that has given me new perspective. Now, in the wake of every storm, I carefully gather the pieces that have survived. I don't expect my individual efforts to withstand the ageless storm but I keep trying and with the proven pieces, I will ultimately build a sanctuary strong and secure for God's people, an oneness with God that can speak hope and promise from the midst of this apocalyptic storm. As difficult a lesson as it has been, I am learning to build in the wind.

STANDING FIRM

The Lord Jesus spoke of our day and said," And because lawlessness will abound the love of many will grow cold. But he who endures to the end shall be saved." (Matt. 24:12&13)

The word endure is an important one prophetically. It is the ability to stand firm in a very tempestuous spiritual environment; one that includes strong opposing winds: the frigid winds of apostasy colliding with the intervening winds of God's fiery discontent; creating a last day's tempest of biblical proportions.

Experiencing success as the world and the worldly church defines it cannot prepare us for Euroclydon. We need revival! The Church was born in the fire of Pentecost. Today, that same fire will revive the church and restore it to its original condition, perspective, and mandate. Only an undying, relentless, even unreasonable pursuit of true revival along with all of its human pitfalls, disappointments, and discouragements can possibly prepare us. The pain of the pursuit has its purpose. It refines those who are called for revival from those who are casual towards it. It further refines those called and separated. Before we can be vessels and voices of revival, we must first be victims of it. Many have recognized the need for revival; others have agreed to the need. Some have even preached the necessity of revival and have on occasion prayed for it. But only those who have lived for it will in the end be willing to die for it. They, like Paul, will stand firm as God's lighthouse in this dark storm.

LIFE SAVING REVELATION

In today's celebrity filled, supercharged religion, being relevant is a continual concern. In order to remain relevant they must be on the cutting edge. Much of what began well has gone askew in its pursuit of new revelation. Unfortunately though, with the pressures of maintaining support bases and budgets, much of what was called revelation was just another angle. I am not suggesting that this 'angle seeking' is done intentionally. It is no less wrong, however; because when the pressures of performance taint our motives, we become vulnerable to false prophecy.

No guessing with the Apostle Paul; he steps forward with a powerful and concrete word from God. In the throws of this howling storm, Paul's heart is filled with solidity and cheer. Note the contrast between his cheer and the others despair. Dripping wet and trembling from the cold, Paul appears as damaged by the storm as any of the others. What's so different about this man? The difference is a divine reality that exists on the inside of Paul. Now the storm has shaken all that can be shaken and reveals the thing which cannot be i.e. Paul's faith in Jesus Christ and God's purpose for Paul. Paul's faith and purpose coupled together make him a vessel of 'life saving' revelation and intervention. Soon our lukewarm religion will realize that 'true revelation' is given to save and perfect the people not to entertain them.

THE SHIP WILL BE LOST

Paul confirms what they are all convinced of; the ship will be lost. Every one of them, though, shall survive the thing none of them expected and can now scarcely believe. Paul was correct in the beginning of this nightmare but is he now? The relentless wind screams otherwise. Perhaps he's guessing or only hopeful.

"The ship will be lost." This normally would mean death to all those aboard especially after so long a time in this punishing storm also taking into consideration the freezing cold and the total fatigue of the men. The intervening hand of God is apparent in the storm.

Paul has received a promise from God which was the salvation of all aboard. The Lord could have saved the ship also but chose not to.

CAN YOU IMAGINE

Can you imagine me saying that structure of the American society, as we know it is about to fall. Can you imagine me saying that this collapse is a product of God's holy discontent with our nation and that he could save the "American Dream" but has chosen not to? Too far fetched huh?

*But wait, could you have imagined New York City without the Twin Towers or much of New Orleans becoming a tourist attraction because of its desolation? Now imagine me saying that the whole complexion of this nation will drastically change before this storm is finished?

Indeed, every thing that can be shaken will be shaken until all that remains standing is faith. It is faith in God that will save the people; the people are the nation! America is in essence an ark rather than a ship and this is what explains the drawing power it has had through the years. The heart of this phenomenon is the Gospel of Jesus Christ. The purpose of the ark, however, has been usurped by the hearts of apostates who have taken upon themselves the installation of sails and rudder and have attempted to steer the nation at their will. These are pirates and not patriots!

The U.S. is not seeing the beginning of the 'last days', it was born into the 'last days' as an ark nation; a nation that would rise above the 'sin that doth abound', a nation that would float, spiritually buoyant, unattached to the sensual self-seeking world below, above, where it's perspective is clear and where it's projection is the 'high road' of God.

It is a nation of Americans whose original dream was not temporal possessions and riches but instead a dream of having absolute freedom to worship God unencumbered by religions and governments who had lost touch with Him. The dream was to live a simple life that would reflect the character of the God they served.

Our nation was founded upon the principles of God Himself those clearly defined and set forth in the Bible. Its foundations, therefore, are heavenly, giving our nation effective buoyancy which has enabled it to rise above its threats. Overloaded with the selfish personal agendas of pirates and heavy anchors of national leaders dragging their feet, refusing to acknowledge the authority of God, it is now unable to rise above our current crisis. God will, therefore, allow the ship to be lost in this God storm. This will give this great nation a fresh start in Christ, a people nation resuming its place as Ark of God to the world.

A PARASITE

The structure of society that I referred to earlier as one certain to collapse is a parasitical one. It does not represent the core of this nation. It is a dark spiritual organism; governed by evil, sensual, unbridled lusts which has attached itself to this nation of people and has fed upon abundant blessing and constitutional freedom. It has grown evil tentacles into every facet of society. This structure will be broken during this God storm. Its destruction will seem as though it is the complete ruin of the nation and that's because of its huge visibility and influence; it's been perpetually promoted on every media but as I said before, it is superficial and it's roots, though incredibly destructive, are also superficial. When it falls, (and I assure it will fall) the true and enduring foundations will be revealed again and the rebuilding will begin. God will be glorified in the process and His ultimate victory will be powerfully conclusive.

The clinging strength of this invading parasite is not merely social acceptance, it is legalization. First there is legalized Abortion, the killing of innocent children within the mother's womb for the sake of convenience, social control, and financial profit. Then there is legalized pornography (in a myriad of unimaginable forms) for the sake of financial profit. Finally there is the progressive legalization of unnatural sexual lifestyles including partnering (with marriage as its ultimate goal) This also includes promotion of these biblically condemned lifestyles to children in schools.

CHAMPIONS

There is overwhelming evidence as to what the motivations of the great founders of this nation were. Their motives were heart felt, righteous, wholesome, and pure. They were champions of all that was good defined by God's word, The Holy Bible. For them, the lines were not blurred; they knew, without a shadow of doubt, what was right and wrong. The genius among these wise men was the favor of God which enabled them to found a nation like none other in the history of the world. God was the foundation and the architect in the hearts of these great men.

Our precious soldiers who have given their lives for liberty have not given them in vain. They have died for the heart of America, for the core of it, for the foundation upon which it stands. America is good and that is what has made her great. It is for that great nation that they have died. They have not died for the evil parasite that clings to it now anymore than they have died for the right to kill American Womb Babies but rather have died to protect them. The magnificent blood of these warriors will soon be vindicated by this God Storm.

PART 7

"And now I exhort you to be of good cheer: for there shall be no loss of any man's life among you, save the ship. For there stood by me this night the angel of God, whose I am, and whom I serve, Saying fear not Paul; thou must be brought before Caesar; and, lo, God has given thee all them that sail with thee." (Acts 27:22-24)

A GIFT TO WHOM?

Please consider this fact. This voyage was not taken specifically for the sake of Paul, at least not from the human perspective. Had Paul not been aboard the ship, the schedules and time frames would have been the same and the identical decisions would have been made. This ship would have been caught up in this crushing storm with or without Paul. The fact that Paul was placed on the ship ultimately became a life saving gift for all those aboard. As chaotic as this situation was, God was still able to save every last soul from a certain death at sea, furthering His purpose and receiving glory at the same time.

This is the ideal end, God's remnant has been praying for. The means to salvation, restoration, or revival we leave totally in God's hands. I know this storm, which is the immovable and inevitable justice of God, will become incredibly difficult but if we are vessels of God's purpose and continually constrained by The Love of God, when this storm reaches its zenith, we will be present and available. At that point, the multitudes will become God's gift to us and we will become life saving gifts to them. This may not be completely perceived by all those involved, never the less, multitudes will be saved and God will be glorified.

NO LOSS OF LIFE

"...fear not Paul", the angel said to Paul. The obvious implication here is that Paul was in a great preoccupation for all the lives aboard the damaged and doomed vessel. Each and every soul held infinite value to the Man of God insomuch as to create a great concern for the welfare of each. The life threatening storm did not create within Paul a new situational concern but instead ignited a passion which had burned in Paul for many years already. It was a love and concern for both the temporal and eternal welfare of all people but especially the eternal. His love was of such sincerity and complete, that the very God of Heaven promised and assured Paul that none would be lost. Alas, God knowing that this would be the only thing which would dispel all fear in the distinct Man of God.

So it will be with us in this last great storm; God will give us the multitudes aboard this wayward and storm beaten nation. Indeed, they will be a gift to us from God when they mean absolutely everything to us representing a value in our hearts so great that the only thing which can give peace is their promised and assured salvation. This divine assurance may not come from an audible voice but it will be a witness so powerful, we will know it to be the Voice of God Himself. The promise will be to those who contain such a passion for the lost that it presents an absolute availability to the Lord. The people will be given to those who are not preoccupied or obsessed with self preservation but moved with a great concern for all those along the way.

NO ENEMY NEAR BY

It's important to reemphasize at this point the danger in allowing ourselves to view the storm as being impersonal. It is not. It still represents the unchangeable holiness and justice of God. It is the raging and impassable vengeance of God; the place where angels dare not tread.

It is the ship and the storm alone. There are no attacking enemy ships involved. The damage they have suffered and the hopelessness they are experiencing is not the result of a successful enemy attack. They've not been thwarted by pirates or criminals at sea. It is the ship and the God Storm alone.

As a servant of God, I am fearfully aware of this one fact; If I allow myself to become narrow minded as it relates to the mechanics of Gods' plan, I will surely fail as an effective tool for His glory. The complexities that exist in our country (including the mountains of secrecy; hidden sins, hidden crimes, hidden agendas, hidden plans, hidden motives) are far beyond the ability of any one person to even comprehend, much less unravel. For me to set out on a personal crusade to prevent the "breaking up" of this wayward ship, would be about as effective as Paul attempting to convince the centurion not to embark on the journey but to wait for spring. Although it will be a long and difficult way, this storm will accomplish Gods' purpose perfectly.

THE PERFECT STORM

The Euroclydon became the unifying factor in the lives of all those aboard the ship no matter how diverse they and their lives were. The dynamics and components of this kind of storm, I do not pretend to know or understand. In fact atmospheric experts are continually discovering new facts about these powerful storms.

Likewise, I cannot pretend to know the components nor understand the dynamics of this Perfect God Storm which is raging in our land even now as I write. No one will transcend the might of this storm; all will be deeply touched by it. It will be the unifying factor in the lives of all of us aboard this American vessel. As this storm continues, the word 'survival' will surface more and more. "Oh Lord...in wrath remember mercy." (Hab. 3:2) I am an incredibly grateful recipient of Gods' mercy and it is still available to all; as for now, however, we will have to discern the voice of mercy flowing from the mouth of Gods' purging discipline.

THE GREATEST OBSTACLE

I have experienced many awesome moves of God which have seemed to be the beginnings of a great revival. All of the necessary spiritual components seemed to be present and wonderfully active. During those times, I was convinced that with such a dynamic presence of God, the revival just could not fail. Although each meeting was wonderfully fruitful and life changing for many, none turned into the prairie fire we'd hoped for. The reason was something I had not expected although I was aware of its dark existence.

The people were blessed beyond measure being carried away by the Glory of God. They seemed to be very responsive to the Word preached; repentance was a welcomed necessity for every type of error until eventually and inevitably the Lord would ask the seekers to put away their idols. It is without a question the most difficult sin to turn away from and to leave at the feet of Jesus. It remains the greatest obstacle to an awakening in our land; it is the chosen slumber above all others.

It is a silent spirit of idolatry within the context of revival which rises up ferociously when it is eventually confronted by the Spirit of Gods' Word. It is an incredibly religious spirit within the Lukewarm and remains harmonious as long as "love for the world and the things of the world" (1John 2:15) is not defined as sin. Once idolatry is exposed as the evil it really is, this spirit will begin to exert control over those bound by it and will quickly create offense, anger, suspicion, controversy, and ultimately scandal in order to destroy the Work of God.

FOOD AND RAIMENT

"And having food and raiment let us be therewith content. But they that will be rich fall into temptations and a snare, and into many foolish and hurtful lusts, which drown men in destruction and perdition. For the love of money is the root of all evil: which while some covet after, they have erred from the faith, and pierced themselves through with many sorrows." (1Tim.6:10)

If we as Americans were reduced to food and clothing alone, it would be considered the end of the world, especially, when our decadence (which has become a way of life) is considered not only a right but a lifestyle well earned. Isn't it interesting that the terrorist attacks were called an attack on liberty? Why then wasn't one facet of the attack aimed at the Statue of Liberty? The message here is spiritual not political. It is not a premeditated message from the terrorists either. That would be giving them too much mental credibility.

THE MESSAGE

The message is from God and it marked the beginning of this great divine intervention. Enemies succeed when defenses are removed or in this case when the Divine Defender has been taken for granted too long. The attack was on 'idolatry' not upon fundamental liberty. The righteous foundations of God have never nor will they ever support the ivory towers of men.

These foundations may be forgotten or taken for granted for a time but (as historic Israel has experienced) will eventually shake all that has been erected upon them. Those structures that have been erected for the glory of man will always crumble.

KNOWING THEM

Much of what is this God Storm will be rejected as being God. "This cannot be God", they will say. "We refuse to believe it!" Few will actually understand what is taking place in the beginning but eventually, more and more will. As things develop, however, the true "enemies of God" will be exposed. How will we recognize them? We will know them by their continued rejection of God's Word, His authority, and His Son Jesus.

PART 8

"Howbeit we must be cast upon a certain island. But when the fourteenth night was come, as we were driven up and down in Adria, about midnight the shipmen deemed that they drew near to some country; and sounded, and found it twenty fathoms: and when they had gone a little farther, they sounded again and found it fifteen fathoms. Then fearing we should fall upon rocks, they cast four anchors out of the stern, and wished for the day." (Acts 27:26-29)

AN ISLAND OF RECONCILIATION

Not aimlessly driven as one would think but rather purposefully driven for there is a specific destination chosen for this ship and passengers. As farfetched and impossible as it might have seemed to the hopeless crew and passengers, The Lord was in complete control.

The belief that all the destruction and human chaos we are experiencing now are purely the consequence of social, economical, or environmental abuse is wrong. Neither is it the result of some mathematical or scientific miscalculation. Adhering to this belief will only prolong the process and increase the pain for our people especially our children. We, as a people nation, must surrender to the fact that God is in control and has chosen a specific destination for this nation, an island of reconciliation. This perfect storm is the consequence of our national wickedness. It lay directly in the path of the course we have chosen. Thank God though; it is not a dead end if we respond correctly to what the Lord is seeking from us. Gods' glorious mercy is in this awful storm. Again, we must respond correctly.

THE MIDNIGHT HOUR

In the early 1960's, prayer was effectively removed from or schools depriving our children of that essential foundation. Eventually those millions of children became the nation, one detached from God. Prayerlessness has detached our people from God and is at the root of our dark and desperate condition. Likewise, this same detachment blinds the people from seeing and recognizing the time, the prophetic time, "the midnight hour"; when God begins to intervene with powerful and dreadful expressions of discontent.

With prayer being exercised by so few, it's no surprise why so few know what is really happening. To find the accurate prophetic consensus, you will have to locate the praying remnant of God; those who are defined by prayer and are well equipped by it for the storm already raging. They are not surprised by it; actually, they have been warning of it for decades. These are those who like Paul have been anchored in Jesus Christ for a long time. They will ultimately teach the hopeless multitudes aboard this doomed vessel how to anchor their souls also in this merciful Christ.

CAST ANCHORS!

It's been determined that the ship is being driven toward land, some island perhaps although they don't know which. The news represents both hope and dread; it could mean their safely going ashore or the ship being destroyed upon rocks and the loss of their lives.

The midnight hour has arrived, the storm rages. What do they do? Do they guess? Do they take a chance and proceed? Will the ship survive the night? Wisely they choose to cast forth the anchors in order to stop the progression of the ship.

The seaman responded correctly to the midnight hour. They chose to stop, to wait… for the light. They would be forced to choose a course; it would more than likely be their last chance at survival; they wanted to choose correctly. "Cast forth the anchors!"

This is exactly how we must respond as a nation to our midnight hour! The choice we make will either mean life or death to our multitudes. We must choose our course carefully and in order to do that we must stop and wait for the light.

LIGHT

Psalm 119:30 says, "The entrance of thy words giveth light; it giveth understanding unto the simple." This is referring to the Word of God or the Bible. This, my friends, is the light we must see and deeply consider before we can successfully proceed in this tempestuous midnight hour. Our consideration of this light will not be tainted by superficial and stupid motivations. We will sincerely consider this light knowing our lives depend upon it.

Let's begin our consideration here: "There is a <u>way</u> which seemeth right unto man, but the end thereof are the <u>ways</u> of death." (Proverbs 14:12) The word way and ways used in this scripture mean; a road, a way, a path. It is essentially a path that has been chosen for a journey to be taken.

There is a consequence to the paths we choose in life; that goes for individuals as well as whole nations. The wrong paths can be devastating and even deadly. The amazing thing about this is that these dead end paths are considered good by those who choose them. As a matter of fact, those who have chosen these deadly paths are so convinced that they are good, they will literally fight in defense of their decision. Unfortunately the end is always the same when the wrong path has been chosen.

DEADLY CHOICES

*As we proceed there will be those who will say," I had nothing to do with these things; I did not agree with the choices; I am not at fault.

Remember, it is Biblical perspective we are considering; from that perspective it is equally wrong when we know what is right and good but fail to do so... In other words doing nothing while wickedness increases is openly condemned.*

Here are a few examples of wrong choices we have made (as a nation of people) that have put us on this path of deadly consequence.

SUFFER THE CHILDREN

The removal of prayer from our public schools in the early 1960s was an incredibly wrong choice and although few people were actually involved in the promotion and legislation for its removal, millions who opposed it stood by and did nothing and have done relatively little to combat the decision since. Of this Jesus said," Suffer little children, and forbid them not, to come unto me: for of such is the kingdom of heaven." (Matthew 9:14) This does not refer just to the individual child praying but the Lord desiring children as a group approaching him. The Lord said to allow the children to come and not to prevent them from coming corporately. This preventing our children from praying in schools is a wrong and deadly choice! If we are to survive this terrible storm, we must reintroduce prayer into our schools and make no mistake about it! It must be prayer to God in the Name of Jesus Christ.

Another incredibly wrong and deadly choice we have made was the legalization of abortion; the killing of an infant human being while in the mother's womb. Approx. 50,000,000 infants have lost their lives as a result of this dark practice. This is not an impersonal issue; these children have been violently killed by other human beings. Can you imagine a type of warfare being waged within our boarders which would claim the lives of one sixth of all Americans; nuclear, chemical, biological? In those terms, it is a staggering consideration!

No single choice that we have made flows more contrary to the foundational principles of our nation and its constitution. The founding fathers could not have imagined such a heinous practice being an everyday part of our society much less supreme court judges finding justification for such a practice within the constitution. Furthermore, what would their commentary be as it relates to the moral condition of the American people who would allow such a thing to continue?

What does the light reveal to us about abortion and what does it require now? While the God Storm relentlessly pounds upon this vessel, let's carefully consider.

The sixth of the ten commandments of God," Thou shalt not kill." (Exodus 20:10) is a word which refers to human life and speaks for itself. It refers to the unnecessary killing of a fellow human being especially the innocent. (Because of the depravity of the human heart, there are times when killing becomes part of the equation based upon defense. This also is clearly defined in the light of Gods' word.) The location or size of a baby does not measure its value or viability. The size of a child in a mother's womb only measures the degree of its innocence, vulnerability, and need to be protected.

The "Womb Child" is socially taken for granted because of the fact that it has no voice. It suffers and dies in silence. But wait; there is a voice that speaks in the behalf of these precious little ones. "And

whoso shall receive one such little child in my name receiveth me."
(Matthew 18:5) Jesus talks about the value of innocent children
and the immense benefit to those who receive them. Jesus used the
word 'receive' which means to receive into ones family, to receive
favorably. This hardly sounds like the treatment an abortion doomed
womb child receives! In essence, The Lord is saying that to reject
the innocent child is the rejection of Him. But the Lords' blinding
light doesn't end there. He continues," But whoso shall offend one
of these little ones which believe in me (referring to child like faith
and character), it were better for him that a millstone be hanged
about his neck, and that he were drowned in the depth of the
sea. (Matthew 18:6) Jesus here implies a dreaded consequence so
horrible it will make this millstone plunge into the depths of the sea
a positive alternative.

No, we cannot move on and expect, with any measure of hope,
to survive this overwhelming storm unless we repent and quickly
bring this awful practice called abortion to an end. The law must be
struck down with the utmost haste. We must ask God to forgive our
perpetrating of this American Holocaust.

I briefly want to affirm that the things we are saying and the
conditions set forth for survival are not up for debate. First of all,
there is no time for debate and secondly all recent debates have been
unfruitful in stemming the tide of wickedness in our nation. There is
not flexibility when it comes to Gods word. It is absolute truth. We
solidly repudiate situational ethics and all social manipulation and
engineering based upon humanistic thought which ultimately turns
into sinful convenience and the empowering of the people to sin
freely and boldly. The Word of God provides practical and merciful

truth all framed within the confines of righteousness.

It grieves my heart when I consider the unfathomable damage done to our children because of the paths we have chosen. Indeed the pain is on going even during this very moment while the storm rages with a fury beyond our greatest imagination threatening our very lives and future. The desperation of the hour (the midnight hour) requires that we leave no stones unturned but that we let the light of God show us the path to life.

SHACKED UP

The controversy over homo-sexual marriage continues to rage and deservedly so. It seems, however, to be gaining acceptance on a daily basis. It is considered to be the greatest threat to traditional marriage in the history of the world; but is it really? No; this biblically condemned reality in our society is only a consequence of something else; it is a back door issue. As much as we would rather blame it wholly for This Perfect Storm, to do so would be a dreadful mistake.

The true villain is one so broadly accepted and almost completely taken for granted and is a two headed monster. This beast has become as much a part of our everyday lives as the wallpaper in our homes. It is divorce and cohabitating ("shacking up" for lack of a more socially understood term).

Nothing has done more to undermine the traditional marriage and family than our out of control divorce statistics. Actually, divorce is a preconditioned option in the minds of most people while saying their wedding vows much like the Wal-Mart promise to accept returned items with no questions asked. Indeed, society's flippant attitude toward the binding power of marriage has produced another incredibly damaging practice and that is "living together". It is the rational conclusion in the minds of multitudes that have seen marriage as merely an unnecessary "piece of paper". "We'll just move in together", they say, and "What's the difference really". Marriage has become a traditional option but not a binding one and to others completely meaningless.

These two exploding bombs have left our nation more unstable than it has been in its history. Divorce and shacking up have done nothing more than to enable adultery, promiscuity, perversion, and pornography which combined have led to the abortions, abductions, and abuses of children in staggering numbers and growing at an unthinkable rate. In this 'sex driven divorce addicted society' very little wholesome and moral commitment is made on the behalf of children.

"Wherefore they are no more two, but one flesh. What therefore God has joined together, let no man put asunder." (Matthew 19:6)

PART 9

"And as the shipmen were about to flee out of the ship, when they had let down the boat into the sea, under colour as though they would have cast anchors out of the foreship, Paul said to the centurion and to the soldiers, Except these abide in the ship, ye cannot be saved. Then the soldiers cut off the ropes, off the boat, and let her fall." (Acts 27:30-32)

ABSOLUTE CONTROL

It's important at this point to once again discuss the nature of this powerful and dangerous storm. Obviously there remain members of this ship crew who have not yet recognized or believed the words of Paul as being related to them from God Himself. As a result of that they cannot know that God is in absolute control.

All attempts to save this great nation of ours must ultimately give way to the unbending, unchanging, infallible Word of God and its concrete steps to salvation whether for the soul of one person or for the soul of an entire nation. All debate and discussion has ended; all that remains as a variable is surrender, not God's but ours. Here are a few who still seek their own means of salvation while the rest desperately wait for 'light'. For these (as with all) there can be salvation only within the confines of God's provision. It requires anchoring the soul in God's promise. Obedience is our anchor and it holds tight even when things seems chaotic and hopeless when it would be easier to run than to stay and pray. There will be an exodus out of this country; many who are able will leave in hopes of finding more security whether financial or physical, however, as difficult as this process will be, the U.S.A will still be the safest place on earth. The reason is, and I repeat, because God is not destroying this great country; He is restoring it to an even greater glory. Those who have left will in the end regret their decision.

REMEMBERING MERCY

"O Lord, I have heard thy speech, and was afraid: O Lord, revive thy work in the midst of the years, in the midst of the years make known; in wrath remember mercy…To perform the mercy promised to our fathers and to remember His holy covenant." (Habakkuk 3:2 & Luke 1:72)

Paul said that except these fleeing men stay aboard the ship, they cannot be saved. There are a couple of things we must see in order to fully understand the necessity of these men staying aboard. First their ultimate salvation hinges upon a promise i.e. a promise given to Paul a man who has given his life totally to a relationship with Jesus which has become deeply intimate. In order to reap the promise you must remain near the Man of God it pertains to. Paul stays on the ship; so must you. Secondly, their ultimate salvation hinges upon a purpose. It is God's purpose for Paul to take this message to Caesar in Rome and nothing will stop God from getting him there. The purpose is in Paul. Paul stays in the ship; so must you stay with the purpose-filled Paul.

The cornerstone of the U.S.A. is a rock solid relationship between the first Americans and the Lord Jesus Christ. Their search was of a land free from the obstacles which hindered them from expressing their love to Him in every facet of life. This land would become a place of covenant even consummation, if you would, where the love between they and their Beloved would come into full fruition. There is no doubt that God was with them. The fruit of that covenant was no less than the birth of the greatest nation the world has ever seen. The promise of God to these early Americans was and is, "Blessed is the nation whose God is the Lord, and the people whom he hath chosen for his own inheritance." (Psalm 33:12)

Now there are many ways of defining America's greatness the one we point out is of course the greatest greatness in its purest form. What defines America's greatness is it's taking of the Gospel to the entire world and it's caring for the poor as the Bible prescribes. All other facets of America's greatness have been given from God as subservient to its Gospel purpose. They have been given in support and in defense of this greater purpose.

The promise and purpose is in the founding fathers and etched in their nation's foundation. It is America's ultimate salvation; to be saved in this God Storm; therefore, you must remain where the purpose and promise are. Woe unto those who have denied or cursed her foundations; unless you repent you will certainly be lost.

And so, as we are face to face with the devastating consequences of our wrong choices, we must cry out to God, "…in judgment remember mercy!"

NO TIME FOR KNOTS

Once confronted by Paul and being warned of certain death, the shipmen respond by cutting off the ropes attached to the lifeboat and letting it drop into the sea. This act was not the removal of their last hope; it meant rather the elimination of all mental alternatives and considerations of rescue other than the God of Paul.

The raging storm coupled with the message that God is their only hope, will convince multitudes also to cut cleanly the ropes of all other considered forms of rescue. Knots require unraveling but at this point there will no longer be any attempt to unravel the circumstances of this problem, there will instead be a surrender to the promise of God as given by those who like Paul have receive the promise of God for the hour.

The cutting of the ropes also represents an acceptance of the fact that there will be no returning to the methods of recent history. Instead of reaching back to the useless and failed methods of carnal and apostate thinking, it will be a reaching back and returning to

God for rescue. Amen. This will set the stage for the greatest soul winning revival this nation or any nation has ever seen.

SELFISHNESS THWARTED

Had these sailors succeeded in their attempt to leave the ship, it would have meant the abandonment of the people in their most desperate and needy hour. But now, having cut away from their selfish pursuits, they could reengage their responsibilities and become part of God's plan to save all those aboard.

At the pinnacle of this God Storm, leaders and skilled workers which are perceived as leaders will finally abandon the selfishness which has made them an object of disdain and distrust among the people of this great nation. They will realize their God given gifts and surrender them for the salvation of this people nation. They will embrace their responsibility as Men and Women of God rather than men and women for themselves. Though they will not save the ship they will bring a greatly helpful and comforting effort to the people.

PART 10

"**A**nd while the day was coming on, Paul besought them all to take meat, saying, this day is the fourteenth day that you have tarried and continued fasting, having taken nothing. Wherefore I pray you to take some meat for this is for your health for there shall not an hair fall from the head of any of you. And when he had thus spoken he took bread and gave thanks to God in the presence of all and when he had broken it, he began to eat. Then were they all of good cheer, and they also took some meat. And we were all in the ship two hundred three score and sixteen souls" (Acts 27:33-37)

THE ULTIMATUM

Fourteen days have passed (most of them spent in expectation of death) now they have reached the end. Will they live or die? While the light begins to dawn the storm rages on; it has out lasted the ship and now an ultimatum has come.

This is how it will be; it has already begun. What will you do with this God Storm America? It will push you until there is no way to avoid the truth. You will be forced to decide. Our sins have led us into this storm and only our repentance will take us out. Reach out to God from the storm and live; …one last chance to choose.

BREAD OF FAITH

Only Paul had heard the voice of the angelic messenger; the supernatural experience was given exclusively to him. The others were still unsure and afraid but Paul's absolute confidence in God was about to change that. Although he could not calm the storm around them he would succeed in calming the one within them. Paul convinced the crew and others to eat after two weeks of having had practically nothing. Immediately their emotions underwent a total change. They felt real joy while they broke bread with Paul but it wasn't because of the food; it was that the Man of God had convinced them that it wasn't their last meal; life would go on for them. This meal was a celebration of the continuation of life not the end of it. Here we see genuine fellowship develop based purely upon faith and it happened not at the end of this storm but during the most dangerous part of it. Remember there are no physical guarantees that any of them will survive this tempest and yet they are experiencing joy, fellowship, and the breaking of bread.

UNINHIBITED ACTIONS

"Eat drink and be merry" pretty much describes this country for the last several decades. We celebrate for a thousand different reasons and sometimes for no reason at all. When piety turned into party, however, things began to fall apart and death began to boldly walk the streets of America. 'Party hardy' became a national past time and that is why the most awful and unthinkable occurrences are reported routinely in our newspapers and televisions everyday.

Daniel 5 tells us a story of a careless king who threw a great party..."for a thousand of his lords, and 'drank wine' in the presence of the thousands." We are safe to say that excess characterized this party. As the party reached a fever pitch something happened and it happens in every party atmosphere. The normal inhibitions of the people are lifted and they begin to do things that they would not usually do. In this case they begin to use the holy vessels of Gods' temple for drinking their own alcohol. What seemed to be no big deal to them was an abomination to God. Suddenly a hand appeared from no where and began to write upon the wall, announcing the destruction of this king and kingdom. Only hours later the warning came to pass! Do you know whose hand it was?

THE WRITING ON THE WALL

Indeed the same hand has now written on the party wall of this great country also. New thinking, progressivism, liberation movements, breaking boundaries, new lifestyles, call it what you will. It is nothing more than the lifting of the natural and healthy inhibitions of the American people in this crazed party atmosphere giving way to the most heinous and unthinkable deeds the world has ever seen.

Look closely. Erratic weather patterns, ever increasing seismic activity, economic turmoil, social chaos, increasing terrorism, uncontrollable drug use, increasing droughts, simply speaking my friends, "The writing is on the wall!"

JOY RESTORED

The difference here is that Gods' purpose in not to destroy America but to restore it to an even greater glory. This terrible God Storm will thoroughly accomplish this purpose. When was the last time we (as a nation) celebrated Gods' salvation and His rescue from catastrophic events and conditions. We will, even before the storm is done. Joy will break forth through out this land and it won't be a result of an economic resurgence or a revival of the 'American Dream' nor will it be for the victory of a great war. Joy filled fellowship and camaraderie will spread across this land and beyond its boarders as a revival of faith in Jesus Christ as Savior and Lord erupts. From that point on the expectations of the people will become more and more positive and even though difficulties will continue for a while longer; there will be a transcending power over all that is dark, foreboding, and evil…it will be, The Joy of The Lord.

NO MORE CRYING

"Then Nehemiah, who was the governor, and Ezra the priest and scribe, and the Levites who taught the people said to all the people, "This day is holy to the Lord, do not mourn or weep." For all the people were weeping when they heard the words of the Law. Then he said to them, "Go, eat of the fat, drink of the sweet, and send portions to him who has nothing prepared; for this day is holy to the Lord. Do not be grieved, for the joy of the LORD is your strength." (Nehemiah 8:9-10)

Here we see a concerted effort by the leaders of Gods' people to encourage them. The people are attempting to recover from the desperate consequence of national sin, in the form of decades of captivity. They have been working to rebuild what their enemies destroyed and it has proven to be a very difficult and dangerous task. They seem to be both physically and emotionally spent when the Law of God is read to them. The reading of this word is a necessary step for the nations rebuilding but now its reading seems to be the breaking point for the people. They are overwhelmed by their own guilt contained within its words and they begin to cry. Although the difficult purging had ended and God was working a great restoration for them; they simply could not realize it. Rubble, ruthless enemies, calloused hands, and guilty hearts is all they could see and feel, so they cried.

Nehemiah, seeing their weeping and realizing the source of it, begins to show them an awesome and transforming truth. He makes no effort to deny the difficulty that exists but rather reveals a greater truth. It is done, finished, completed; God has delivered them from their enemies. It is not a time for mourning; it is a time for rejoicing; a time for jubilee. Not only are they delivered from their enemies, they are also forgiven. It's time to stop crying and to start celebrating! The fullness of victory and rebuilding could not be seen, as a matter of fact, nothing really changed for the moment but the hearts of the people began to immediately change as they began to experience the Joy of the Lord. Indeed, Gods' victory and salvation in every situation is a foregone conclusion to all those who embrace Him and place their trust in Him. It will be no different for America, when at the end of this Storm, she recommits herself to Jesus Christ her foundation.

PART 11

"And when they had eaten enough, they lightened the ship, and cast out the wheat into the sea". (Acts 27:41)

DAD'S PASSION

It was 1963. My father had been injured in a car accident and for a whole year was unable to work. He, being a farmer, knew when spring came it was time to work, time to plow the ground and sow the seeds. It was in his blood. Dad couldn't work and was forced to depend upon others to do it for him. He was absolutely miserable. He actually developed an ulcer and nearly bled to death at one point. As you might imagine, dad was climbing onto tractors and using a shovel way earlier than he was supposed to.

Dad had a tremendous work ethic and if I learned anything from him, it was how to work. As a boy, I struggled with much of the work even hating some of it. It was just work to me. I really didn't see the purpose. Dad had an absolute focus ... the harvest. Each job we did was important in the progression of producing the harvest. With each passing day, more of my father's life was invested in that year's crop. It was his life's passion.

I remember his emotional intensity and how it would increase as the summer passed by. He seemed hard even harsh at times. There were moments when I didn't like dad at all; I couldn't relate. Dad's gone now. He died of cancer in 2000 but I love and appreciate him now more than ever just simply because I understand his work better and of course his heart for the harvest.

When that final load of golden harvest had been delivered, everyone breathed a sigh of relief and a spirit of celebration seemed to fill the house. Oh the value of the precious wheat.

FINE FROM A DISTANCE

There is always risk with harvest. One particular year, late in August, a heavy storm passed over our wheat crop. The storm brought hail, enough hail to beat some of the leaves off the trees which were in the yard. Dad didn't know haw badly the wheat was damaged by the storm. I could see the concern in his face. I, on the other hand, did not feel the same concern; I was just a kid and had no concept of the value of the wheat. I was the 'son of a harvester' not one myself not yet anyway. I had nothing invested, and so, nothing to lose. I asked Dad if we should take the combine out to the wheat. He said we would have to wait a couple of days for the crop to dry out; we would know then. He would walk off and begin doing something else but I knew he was worried.

I knew how to operate the combine and was proud of it; in fact, the crop was just an excuse to running the big machine. After two days, we went out to the field to give the wheat a try, and yes, I was running the machine. As I approached the field, the wheat looked fine. I was glad! It didn't seem damaged by the hail at all. I lowered the platform and began to cut the grain. The straw was heavy promising a good yield; however, almost no grain was coming into the bin. I wondered what was wrong! Perhaps a hole had been worn in the sheet metal somewhere and the grain was escaping through it. I stopped to check but could see no leaks. It was at that point, while kneeling on the ground, when I realized what had happened. I saw the grains of wheat scattered everywhere like pearls in the dirt. I was shocked; no wonder there was no grain coming into the tank. It was all on the ground.

The wheat stalk had not been damaged by the hail but almost all the grain had been knocked onto the ground. The wheat remained standing even though the grain was lost. From a distance the wheat had looked fine now I could see it had been lost in the storm.

Oh America, how our decisions have hurt us! Our neglect of the harvest has cost us so very much. Now when we really look, we see that almost all has been lost. From a distance we have appeared to be fine but honest and close scrutiny reveals a whole generation lost, strewn like pearls upon the ground of our evil neglect.

WHAT NOW?

"What will we do now", I asked my dad. "We'll string electric fence around the entire field', he replied, "And then turn the hogs out on it. They will recover quite a bit of the grain." In my boyish way of thinking I thought, "If there was just a giant vacuum cleaner big enough to suck up all the wheat, but not the pigs! The pigs will ruin it!"

Is that what we as a nation are going to do; allow the pigs of immorality, injustice, hatred, murder, neglect, selfishness, greed, and (as it relates to our children) abductions, abuse, and abortions to totally destroy our great nation?!

A new mentality is the only way; knowing that doing good is right and doing right is good based upon God's Word, the Bible.

STUPID PIG

I watched the pigs root around that field for weeks until not a seed of wheat was visible. Most of it was just packed into the muddy ground and wasted.

There is a pig mentality you know. Let me tell you about it from a farmers / preachers perspective. It is the willingness to sacrifice the innocent for selfish reasons including money, convenience, political agendas, and evil appetites.. It is the merchandising of our children. Let me show you an amazing and horrifying example.

Hog production had been a large part of our family farming for many years. Much of our labor had to do with the pigs. Among 150 sows was one sow in particular. She was scary and problematic and as a result was made into bacon earlier than usual. Dad warned us kids to stay away from her. She was mean and aggressive. In the beginning she was a good producer of piglets too, but suddenly turned bad.

The last bunch of piglets she bore, she ate, as quickly as they were being born. We were all amazed to see what she had done but we couldn't figure it out at first. It was obvious she had had the babies but we couldn't find them. Finally Dad saw the blood around her mouth and knew what she had done. Now these were well fed animals yet she had eaten her own offspring! "What a stupid pig", I thought!

THE SOUND OF WORSHIP?

Does what this sow did shock you? It did me but let me tell you something more shocking still. The similarities are devastating. Did you know that the physical remains of aborted children and the by-products of abortions are often processed (called protein or collagen...among other names) and used as ingredients in cosmetics then marketed and reapplied onto the skin of a generation of consumers who are aborting children by the thousands almost everyday. The nature of the rogue ...the pig mentality!

Papa warned us all, "Don't ever feed the pigs raw meat of any kind; they will develop a taste for blood and become dangerous!" How right my dad was.

Polls indicate that approx. 90 per cent of Americans call themselves Christians. So be it; but let me tell you something else.

As long as this horrible sin is casually accepted or easily tolerated, no true worship can be offered to God with the exception of a pure and praying remnant who hates this sin as they love their God.

Long ago, written in the history of Israel an incident took place which further sheds light upon our desperate times. In the holy temple of God (which stood in the city of Jerusalem), a pig was offered upon the altar. It was done by one Antiochus Epiphanes an enemy of Israel who had set up worship to a false god of his choice. He was ultimately defeated by a courageous family who led the way to his overthrow. Nevertheless, can you imagine the screams of this pig while it is being drug into the temple and then hoisted up and killed upon the altar? Not the sound of worship the LORD wants to hear. But what do you suppose much of our worship sounds like as long as this heinous sin is allowed to continue in our land. You hit the nail on the head.

KERNELS OF LIFE

The final step to lightening the ship was taken when the wheat was thrown overboard. This does not mean that the wheat was taken for granted but just the opposite instead. Earlier the ship had been lightened with extreme measures when even the tackling of the ship was discarded. The fact the wheat was left till last indicates the conclusion among them that the wheat was the most valuable of all.

Within this desperate context, the wheat represents three basic things. These three things must be recognized as the most important and valuable subjects in our nation. All effort must then be directed toward them.

Wheat is of itself seed. The seed represents the Words of God or the Holy Bible...its promotion...its study... and its application as absolute authority.

The baked product of milled wheat is bread. The bread represents the acceptance, the love, and the adoration of Jesus Christ as the Bread of Life and the only Savior of the World.

Again we consider the seed aspect of wheat in the most practical way. We must accept the unspeakable value of our children from conception as precious seeds of our future. No less valuable are our elderly who must be embraced as precious seeds of our eternity, one our destiny the other our legacy.

We are told that the wheat was not discarded until all had eaten and were full. After days of fear and hunger, they were now prepared to fight for life. This nation will be well on its way to recovery only when we have heard and fully accepted the value of the wheat I have just described. We have discarded our kernels of life for too long. Oh the value of the Wheat.

PART 12

"And when it was day, they knew not the land: but they discovered a certain creek with a shore, into the which they were minded, if it were possible, to thrust in the ship. And when they had taken up the anchors, they committed themselves unto the sea, and loosed the rudder bands and hoisted up the main sail to the wind and made toward shore. And falling into a place where two seas met, they ran the ship aground; and the forepart stuck fast, and remained unmovable, but the hinder part was broken with the violence of the waves." (Acts 27:39-41)

A NEW PLACE

The people have been blown into a position where they can finally be saved from what seemed to be certain death. Only hours before they had totally given up on ever escaping this tremendous storm. The journey has been terrifying and though they have a promise of complete escape it will not be without effort.

When the greatly anticipated morning finally brings light, they find themselves in a place they don't recognize. Everything they see is new to them. Obviously this course is not one they would have plotted. Out of the way, out of the ordinary, not a place they would have chosen to be. They had planned to winter at Phenice but hardly expected to end up here.

Oh how I have hungered to faithfully serve and follow Jesus. My pursuit of Him has been far from occasional or casual; it has been a lifestyle. It hasn't been without its challenges though. I guess it's partly because my pursuit is of Jesus Himself not Jesus as a means to success or a fulfillment of goals. There are those who have been very successful <u>with</u> the name of Jesus but not <u>in</u> the name of Jesus. My effort has been to be <u>constantly in</u> Jesus not <u>occasionally with</u> Jesus. In order to follow hard after the Lord, I've had to remain focused. The way is strait and because of that I've had to learn a lifestyle of repentance. And that lifestyle, just like these folks on this ship, has taken me places I would have never gone on my own.

Right now, this God Storm is driving our country to a place it has never been before. Soon she will look around and find that everything she is seeing and experiencing is new.

PERSONAL SHIPWRECK

I can't remember all the many times the storms of consequence have driven me to a place of repentance. I have often prayed, "God purify me and deliver me from hypocrisy..." It wasn't long after that the wind would begin to blow. I had (and probably still do) so many misconceptions and blind spots that were grieving the Holy Spirit. These things were hindrances to my intimacy with the Lord. I desperately wanted them removed and the Lord has helped me with my own private and personal storms. I wish I could say that I have grown on my own but no...the Lord has blown me to the necessary places of repentance and I praise Him for it. My heart breaks with each personal shipwreck but when repentance is accomplished, the Lord always gives me another boat to continue my journey with Him.

Obviously the dimension of what God is doing in the U.S. is much greater but the motive, nature, and purpose are the same. God loves this nation but His relationship with her did not begin with us, it began with her founders. His commitment to restore her is on behalf of the founders' dedication of commitment to Him...the God of the Bible. God is the storm; therefore, within the heart of this tempest there is perfect love, peace, and wisdom. This wisdom knows exactly how far to push America to reach her place of repentance. Yes it will be a place totally different from what she has known and been accustomed to in her history, especially in her recent past.

THE NARROW GATE

Not knowing this place does not deter the men. They know that their lives depend on reaching its shore. This island is their only hope and this moment is their last chance to reach it. The sails are lifted while the anchors are cut away. Their aim is to pass through a narrow alley way that they have discerned; perhaps through it they can reach the shore and live.

"Enter ye in at the strait gate; for wide is the gate, and broad is the way, that leadeth to destruction, and many be which go in thereat; Because strait is the gate, and narrow is the way, which leadeth unto life, and few there be that find it. (Matt.7:13-14)

In this word, Jesus says that many will choose a path that leads to destruction where as only a few will choose a path that leads to salvation and life. "The many" and "the few" comprise the whole or everybody; there are no exclusions here. It takes no effort to find the wide gate all you need to do is follow "the many". The narrow gate, on the other hand, requires what only "the few" are willing to do... searching for it with sincerity, honesty, and brokenness. Once the narrow gate is found, there must be a focused and committed effort to enter through it.

The order to cut away the anchors and to hoist the main sails was given. This meant an all out commitment to the sea in order to reach the goal.

There can be no half-hearted attempts at finding truth unto salvation! You must completely commit yourself to it. What is the truth; the truth about God and equally important, the truth about you. You must cut away the anchors of denial and all the other things which have held you back to this point. Settle it in your heart just as these sailors did; now is the time, no turning back! This we speak to all diversity of peoples and spiritual conditions; this is the only gate, narrow and absolute truth. The word 'narrow' relates to the unspeakable value of this entrance and also of its inaccessibility to those who are not absolutely serious and desperate seekers of it. This is not a gate which is found at a whim! Multitudes perish everyday for a lack of heart...the heart to find this narrow gate.

The narrow alley they had committed to only took them so far, suddenly it became shallow and the ship was ran aground.

This my friends is where it gets serious. This is where the rubber meets the road. Men can produce the fruits of strong emotion but only God can produce fruits unto repentance; as I said before, Only God can push us just hard enough and just far enough. Remember their lives are depending on it.

So is yours and so is ours as a nation. The lane became shallow and they couldn't proceed, likewise, if our effort is shallow our progress will end here.

To proceed unto life, there must be a deep conviction of sin and a deep appreciation of what Jesus accomplished for us on the Cross. "Jump into the sea" They commanded them. Yes jump into the deeper waters of truth and confession. Jump into the deeper waters where you are completely immersed in the cleansing power of Jesus' blood. Jump into the deeper waters of true deliverance and into the depths of God's grace where you can freely swim unto the shore of eternal life. Don't let the attitudes of a shallow world, a shallow people, a shallow religion stop you. Don't trade this for some half hearted, sinful, lukewarm, and benign existence. Jump in and swim for the shore!

CHANGED FOREVER

Those who successfully pass through this narrow gate are changed forever, transformed. Just beyond it they are embraced by all those who have experienced the same supernatural change. Then, looking back at the narrow gate, they perceive it as a womb and they themselves as new people..."born again."

A LOOK BACK

Can you imagine seeing these people as they finally reach the shore? Dripping wet, trembling and exhausted, some staggering others dragging themselves but all are absolutely alive just as Paul had promised. Then one by one they turn and look back at the ship where they have spent the last two weeks wondering if they'd live another day. In the howling wind they watch the sea violently tearing the ship apart and wonder in amazement how they survived.

Americas survival and restoration will be totally amazing second only to what God has done in beloved Israel. It will be attributed to the supernatural power of God, thus He will be acknowledged and praised in the glorious atmosphere of revival that will prevail during Americas greatest hour.

Even then, the people will look back at this nation torn and ravaged by this awesome and dreadful God Storm and wonder how they have survived. But there will be no grieving for what has been broken but instead a rejoicing for what has been saved. "America… The People" are saved; her foundations have remained strong.

PART 13

"And the soldiers counsel was to kill the prisoners, lest any of them should swim out, and escape. But the centurion, willing to save Paul, kept them from their purpose..." (Acts 27:42-43a)

I assume that these prisoners, like Paul, were on their way to be tried in a court of law and perhaps some of them would be convicted and perhaps some might even be condemned to die but certainly not yet.

The idea to kill them would surely keep them from escaping, cruel and evil as it might be; perhaps fear of reprisal by "higher ups" caused the soldiers to think this way. Maybe they hoped that this type of rigid action would gain them respect within this military of known competitiveness and cruelty.

ULTIMATE PRISON

The point is, had the decision of the soldiers stood, all of these prisoners would have been killed and Paul probably would have been included. What these prisoners would have done with their lives bears no significance upon the decision the soldiers had agreed upon. "Let's put them in the ultimate prison, their own graves. We can't have them escaping, it would reflect on us and that would be a problem." From their perspective, it must have been a viable option because, all though the centurion stopped the soldiers, there is no record of a rebuke or reprimand toward them for their intended course of action. The prophetic accuracy of Paul coupled with the obvious Grace of God resting on his life had convinced the centurion to allow the Man of God to live and all the others along with him.

PRECIOUS DECISION

There is no greater crime than to steal an individuals' future. Death is the absolute way of accomplishing that end. If we were to ask a number of people," What is the one greatest opportunity in a person's entire future?" We would receive a diversity of answers.

Before we proceed any further, let's avoid being distracted. The perspective we cling to, because of its power to save us and our nation, is Gods'. The truth of the Bible and God's perspective contained within its pages is the perspective we mean.

The eternal souls of the people were Paul's priority all along. At this point, Paul has essentially saved all those aboard this ship from certain death at sea. He also rescued the prisoners from certain death from a secondary source, the soldiers in charge of them.

Whether these people had heard the Gospel from Paul at this point is debatable. (I don't think so but I may be wrong.) The one thing that is certain, however, is that every one of them, because they are alive, still retains the opportunity to hear the Gospel and 'decide' whether to receive or reject it. The value of this choice transcends all possible opportunities that any future can produce! Therefore, to rob this decision from anyone is the greatest crime, the crime that reverberates in eternity.

Now, given the opportunity to choose, knowing that many will reject the Gospel, let's consider those who would have accepted it. The killing of those individuals not only robs them of accepting Christ but also of the opportunity of living the remainder of their lives on His behalf.

SO MANY...

The ramifications of this heinous crime go nuclear when we consider the 'womb children' killed through abortion. These are certainly included among those robbed of this priceless opportunity to choose. We must further consider that simply because of the sheer numbers of 'womb children' killed that a huge number of them (had they been allowed to live to adulthood) would have accepted Jesus as Savior. Furthermore, among that number would have been the Anointed of God, those being, great men and women (similar to Paul) dispatched specifically for such a time as this. Can you imagine a child sitting on the lap of Jesus, longingly peering into His eyes and saying, "I love you Lord and thank you for receiving me here; I only wish I could have lived to adulthood and have served you down there".

If you are in a place of authority and have supported abortion or have been indifferent toward it, or have voted for people who do support it, repent quickly. The hammer of God's accountability is about to fall and you do not want to be under it when it does! Like the centurion who recognized the power of God and stopped the killing so must you do! Now!

NOT OUR OPTION

I recently heard a doctor speaking to a patient after she had undergone a pregnancy test and a general exam. He told her that she was indeed pregnant and that both she and the baby were healthy. He went on to say that at this point she had a couple of options: she could carry the baby to full term or she could terminate the pregnancy. He continued by telling that if she chose to continue the pregnancy and changed her mind later, that terminating the pregnancy would still be an option.

We've discussed this "priceless choice" given to us from God as unalienable.

Therefore our response to this pig mentality is, "No, the choice is not with the mother or anyone else! The choice is with the womb child'.

PART 14

"**B**ut the centurion…commanded that they which could swim should cast themselves first into the sea, and get to land: and the rest, some on boards, and some on broken pieces of the ship. And so it came to pass, that they escaped all safe to land." (Acts 27:43b-44)

SLUMPING

It was in Yuma Arizona in October of 1991. We were preaching in a small church where the Lord's moving was wonderfully tangible. The people were experiencing the presence of God in an intimate way, a way they were not accustomed to. They were being blessed and so were we. Yet in the midst of this Cordalee (my precious wife) and I found ourselves fatigued and weary. This was the third year we had lived full-time in the R.V. Cordalee cared for me and our three boys also guiding them through their home schooling everyday all the while within the confines of the small trailer.

We reached this place of weariness from time to time during the twelve years we lived in the R.V. In it, we became impatient and short with one another but it never lasted long; we knew how to over come it. On this particular occasion, we slipped away from the boys for an unusual mid-afternoon slice of cherry pie at a near by Village Inn. Once back at the R.V., I took the next necessary step in overcoming this "human slump"; one I had taken countless times before.

ALONE WITH GOD

The pastor had given me a key to the church building, should I need anything or just to come in to pray. It was about 4:30 that afternoon when I went into the building to seek and wait upon the Lord. Mom and the boys seemed secure so I felt at peace going in. It wasn't long until I felt engulfed by the Glory of God. This is the place where I have found my solutions. There is a renewing there which is impossible for me to describe. My joy, my out-look, my anticipation and expectations of the Lord absolutely soar when coming out of this Womb of Gods' Spirit! All of the sudden, It was well into the night!

I decided to turn a light on, letting my family know I was still inside and ok. Then I returned to the Lord. The sanctuary was dimly lit as the Presence of God went to another level. Up to this point, to me, the Lord had communicated prophetically many times and these messages (through the various forms that He had chosen) had been amazingly accurate. On this night the Lord chose to share another message with me.

While I was staring into the back wall of the room, I began to see some type of motion. At first I thought that perhaps it was just me; I vigorously blinked my eyes and continued to pray. It became clearer and appeared to be some type of movement behind a lattice but then the vision cleared and I could see that I was passing over this great nation of ours as though I was flying or being carried. Suddenly we came upon a large city. It was incredibly devastated. There was destruction everywhere but I could not tell what had caused the destruction, although it seemed to me that it was of a natural cause, ironically what folks would call an "act of God". Then I was taken to another city which had suffered the same fate.

Although I hadn't seen the Lord, it was at this point that, by His Spirit, He spoke to me. "Do you recognize this city?" I said to the Lord that I did not recognize it at all. He went on to tell me that it was a city I knew with in this country of ours. The extent of the ruin seemed almost complete! Remember this was a vision, spiritually prophetic. There was an amazing calm even in the midst of the destruction. I saw no burning buildings. I heard no crying people or children. I heard no siren screaming. I saw no one at all.

PRAISES EVERYWHERE

Leaving that place and on the move again, I began to realize how wide spread the destruction was. Then moving out toward the suburbs I began to see some people moving about; then more and more of them. There were signs of rebuilding everywhere. I saw none of this in the city but out here life seemed to be springing up everywhere. The most amazing part of this vision was what I saw and heard next. There were small groups of people; many of them in different places singing praises to God. As the Lord took me from place to place, there were people praising God everywhere. In parks, in parking lots, on street corners, in the country side; praises to our Lord were going up everywhere. The air seemed clean not free of pollution but of sin and an absence of fear was evident. It was awesome…then suddenly an immense flash of light and the vision was over.

I am not sure exactly what happened causing so much destruction but one thing I am sure of was that the Lord is in complete and absolute control and that there is no reason to fear when we are secure in Him; when we are His and He is ours.

Like all those who escaped the raging storm and looked back to see the destruction of the ship so will the multitudes do right here in this great country as they too look back at the destruction the God Storm has wrought. Nevertheless, in the end, God will have accomplished the greatest restoration of a gentile people the world has ever seen. Yes; many things will be broken but from the rubble will come forth life; the darkness will have fled and America will be greater than ever.

AN INCONVENIENT TRUTH?

Will people die during this time? Obviously Gods' primary goal is to save souls from the suffering of eternal damnation in Hell. In the

Bible, eternal separation from God is death. In this sense, my answer would be this: Those who die are only those who refuse to live. In other words, they are the ones who refuse to do what is necessary in order to receive eternal life and that is to repent (change their minds) and to forsake their sinful and wicked ways. Seem primitive to you? Well, truth has become such an alien concept in this country that it too seems primitive. The fact remains, this is the only way.

The three imperatives this incredible God Storm will accomplish are these:

Sweeping revival across this great land and in it multitudes of Americans receiving salvation.

Gods' obvious defense and vindication of the sacred covenant made between He and the Founders, the words of which are woven throughout the many documents which define and ensure our freedom.

The Bible once again recognized as absolute truth.

THE SURVIVORS

There were three means used by the people when escaping the doomed ship. Again, from a prophetic perspective, let's discuss three groups of people which the three means of escape represent.

The first group consists of the ones who entered into the cold waters first. They were the ones who "could swim". Now the word could refers to the physical strength of the individual. These are the ones who were able to swim to the shore on their own strength. These are the ones of an extraordinary sort, the ones who stand-out during difficult times. After two weeks of tremendous stress and strain, exposure and hunger, they are still able to swim to land.

These swimmers represent the remnant of God; the ones who have recognized the direction our country is going in and have chosen a different course for themselves. They are in touch with the Heart of God and thus informed as to what lies ahead for our land. They are the ones who have separated themselves from the currents of the world and are self-sufficient In Christ. These are the ones who are strong and prepared for the storm.

The second group of people were those who although probably knew how to swim were simply too weak to do so. They were able to escape upon boards. The word boards, used here, would probably identify them as being from the ships deck. They are also called planks which in our terms describes them as being very heavy, wide, and long which they were. They are abundantly used building timbers in the construction of the ship. These boards would easily support the weight of a person clinging to it.

Those clinging to these decking timbers or, otherwise, construction timbers represent those who are either deeply religious whose religion is based upon the Bible or those who are actual Christians who have been saved by faith in Jesus and washed in the Blood of Jesus but have grown lukewarm.

In both cases, they are occupying themselves in the building plans of their own desires and makings. Their priorities are their own personal goals and achievements. They are not necessarily rich nor are their pursuits of finance alone although finance is the dominant motivation. They justify these pursuits with the Bible and are affirmed by a lukewarm status-quo which comprise the majority of those most visible. These too will be saved clinging to the remnants of a misguided religious life.

The third group of people who miraculously reach the land are those who did so clinging to "broken pieces of the ship". This is referring to floating debris most likely actual wooden parts being broken off the ship by the violent waves.

These represent the largest group of people who will be involved in this last great revival. They are the multitudes who are neither saved nor Biblically religious. They are the people who will hear the Gospel message preached, will believe it, and will whole heartedly accept it unto eternal life. These are those who will reach the land clinging to the broken pieces of their lives. It will be a huge number of precious souls who will dance upon the shores of God's infinite mercy and grace.

These three groups combined will be the restored United States of America.

They will raise the Stars and Stripes again, indeed, they will hoist Old Glory high in the American sky and they will do it for the Glory of God! Hallelujah.

PART 15

"But as the days of Noah were, so shall also the coming of the Son of Man be. For as in the days before the flood they were eating and drinking, marrying and giving in marriage, until the day Noah entered into the ark, and they knew not until the flood came, and took them all away, so shall also the coming of the Son of Man be...and (God) spared not the old world, but saved Noah the eighth person, a preacher of righteousness, bringing in the flood upon the world of the ungodly,...Which sometime were disobedient, when the longsuffering of God waited in the days of Noah, while the ark was in preparing, where in few, that is, eight souls were saved by water." (Matt 24:37-39; 2Peter 2:2; 1Peter 3:20)

THE PROBLEM

I recall how that after my salvation, I was so very interested in the study of future events found in the Book of the Revelation. As time went by, I found that this is often the case with new converts to Christ Jesus. Mine, in the beginning, was a human interest filled with intrigue and curiosity but not really understanding the gravity of the human toll these apocalyptic events would take nor did I realize the dense and determined spiritual warfare that would be waged during those culminating moments in history. It was scary of course but seemed somehow sci-fi-ish and alien to what I was seeing and hearing in the church. At church there seemed to be no real concern for these types of things ,as a matter of fact, the atmosphere and attitude of the whole process seemed to dismiss these dire realities rather than to prepare for them. Not much has changed really and it's not that the people are unaware of these things; it's just that the awareness is not creating within them the preparedness necessary. My heart has always burned with a prophetic awareness and intensity but I have also experienced the tendency to be less of 'the watchmen' than these super desperate times demand. What then is the problem?

ARK BUILDER

It appears that Noah was involved in agriculture prior the Lord coming to him with this drastic word of warning. This meeting with God turned Noah's world up side down. What ever Noah had done prior to that moment immediately changed; he was now an ark builder and he would be for approximately a century.

When the prophetic realities concerning our nation are quickened within the hearts of the people, their priorities will also change. They too will become ark builders regardless of what they were before. Preparation will be a daily priority as they see the clouds gathering.

EIGHT AMONG MULTITUDES

I can only imagine the whirlwind of thoughts and emotions that Noah was experiencing. Noah was the 'Man of God', a lover of righteousness and a preacher of it. Because of the special nature of this man, his passions had to have been far more intense than most can conceive of. His track record was clear. His standards were high. His witness was "perfect among his generation".

He was a choice man; a man among men; determined to serve God. Having considered all of these things, I cannot believe that after all was said and done, that Noah expected that there would only be eight people aboard the ship! No way…impossible!

WHY?

There is a terribly disconcerting fact about all of this. A fact that none of us can afford to ignore. Jesus said, "As in the days of Noah so shall also the coming of the Son of Man be." In doing so, the Lord prophetically attached that time of history with ours. The statement is as immutable as God Himself. It will certainly develop and come to pass, therefore, in order to prepare for its reality; we need to first understand its meaning.

Denial is a huge hindrance in implementing this lifesaving work. Can you imagine Noah, rationalizing this whole spiritual encounter with God then dismissing it as being too far fetched? Someone just recently told me, "These things won't come in my life time nor in my grandchildren's!"

Amazing! Yet denial is not the only interfering issue. It is actually under girded by something else. The Bible teaches us that it took Noah approximately 100 yrs too complete the construction of the ark. During this entire time, life continued as it had before Noah's encounter with God, at least with everyone except Noah and his family. The Word of God states that The Lord was very patient with this wicked generation of people while Noah was working to complete this decades consuming project.

As time went on, the work of Noah probably became routine to on lookers or passersby. The sounds of his labors and the declarations of his messages had grown predictable, part of the landscape, if you would.

Finally, God's word began to come to pass. After being miraculously drawn, the animals were loaded. Then with the securing of Noah's family with in the salvation vessel; God closed the door. The rains came and the waters began to rise. Incredibly the Bible points out to us that, "the (people) knew not until the flood came and took them all away." The point is that the people did not understand nor grasp the desperate reality of the situation. They did not understand the reality of their accountability to God. They did not realize the consequence of sin. And they dismissed everything that Noah was saying, and doing, as being too insignificant to respond too and so they didn't... and so they died. They were surprised to death even though every thing necessary to be saved was right before their eyes.

USELESS EFFORTS

This same God Storm which Noah's generation experienced was also a foregone conclusion. It was smack dab in the path their evil hearts had chosen to follow and there was no way for them to overcome it other than aboard Noah's Ark. Now it's too late; the door is closed and the waters are rapidly rising. Do you think now they are convinced of the necessity of an ark? Not immediately at least.

The natural thing to do, which I am convinced many of them did, was to head for the high ground. Up the hills and onto the mountains while the rain relentlessly fell and as the water continued to rise. The Bible says, however, that this was to no avail because the waters rose far above the highest mountain.

We are seeing the same efforts being made today in our country. Many believe that somehow we can overcome this strong storm. "Determination and hard work you know, we've done it before!" People are looking to mountains of finance, to mountains of education, to mountains of social manipulation, to mountains of religion, to mountains of political reform, and many more yet they are not the answer; the waters of the storm will rise far above man's ability to overcome.

NORMALCY

What was the thing that so deceived that generation of people? It is the same thing that is deceiving many today and will deceive you also if you let it.

It is normalcy!

The Lord prophetically said this to me and He did so nearly two decades ago… "There will be a strong message of normalcy preached in your land. When you here it, my strong intervention will have already begun. When you hear that message, know this, nothing will ever be normal again and the end will be near".

It was shortly after the twin towers had fallen. Our enemies were boasting and the world was wondering. At that point it was determined by our leadership that "America must resume our normal lifestyles". We simply could not allow our enemies to think that they had disrupted our entire country. We would be "unmoved"! This message of normalcy continued for months and it was what the Lord had said would come. We have learned since, however, that nothing will ever be the same again.

Imagine the sentiments of the people in his day, "Noah has been at this for a long time and all remains the same. The sun rises and sets. The birds continue to sing. The children continue to laugh. The bride and groom continue to marry. Nothing has changed; all remains the same." They concluded that Noah was wrong; but history proves that they were wrong, dead wrong. <u>Normalcy stopped their ears to the message Noah preached; while denial drowned their hopes of ever boarding the ark.</u>

NOW'S THE TIME

We are in a storm! It is the God Storm! The Ark is Jesus Christ of the Bible and the time is now. There is no other way to be saved. Any other means, whether the solutions of men or of gods, are lies. Be humble and repent. Then together we will pray, "God have mercy on this great nation of ours".

"Be it known unto you all, and to all the people of Israel, that by the name of Jesus Christ of Nazareth, whom ye crucified, whom God raised from the dead, even by him doth this man stand here before you whole. This is the stone which was set at nought of you builders, which is become the head of the corner. Neither is there salvation in any other: for there is none other name under heaven given among men, whereby we must be saved." (Acts 4:10-12)

NICE BUT FALSE

I mentioned in an earlier segment, my dad's battle with cancer, the battle he ultimately lost. It lasted a couple of years, very difficult years. I remember the night my mother informed me about dad's disease. It was a weird feeling almost surreal; I could hardly believe it. It was a week or so before I saw Dad after learning of his condition. He was standing in the carport when I drove up. He didn't look sick, maybe a little weak is all but not really sick. I hugged him and we prayed.

Dad underwent difficult surgery and was very encouraged afterwards even though the doctor told us that he couldn't remove all of the disease. It wasn't long and Dad was up and around doing the things he felt he had to get done. He felt well but was struggling with the changes the surgery had brought.

Less than a year later, he began to go down hill again. The symptoms had returned; Dad was hurting pretty bad but he was tough; he never complained. The doctor said that he had a very strong heart and that it would take him far. The doctor was right. The disease invaded his entire body before it took my Papa down. As things progressed, the doctor informed us of changes to expect.

Dad attended church regularly but became super excited during one of those meetings and told us about it a couple of days later. During the latter part of the service there seemed to be a culminating moment. At that moment, someone whom Dad greatly trusted and respected, came to Dad and told him that God had healed him of this disease and that everything was going to be all right. Dad held to that word. The word was nice but it was false.

SIN SICK

Listen carefully. Sin is the cancer that is ruining our nation; it is the reason we are in this predicament. The disease has reached every area of this nation's body. There are no exceptions; it is sin sick from the very bottom to the very top. Just as the doctors told us that day, it has invaded the entire body.

Papa received a very nice prophecy from a very nice person

who had good motives; but they were wrong. There are also good people with good motives (people you trust and respect) who are prophesying full recovery for America. But they too are wrong. Until the cancer of sin is dealt with, there will be no recovery.

DON'T WAIT

The surgeon said that had Papa come in sooner, he could have recovered but unfortunately, he had waited to long. He had been feeling bad for a while but we couldn't convince him to see a doctor.

I tell you these things in honor of my Dad and in hopes that you and I won't make the same mistake. Let us surrender to God now, while there is still time. Let's pray and listen to God who knows instead of all those who do not. Some of the voices out there are sincere while others have dark and evil motives; either way, they are all wrong unless they too are saying, 'It is time to return to God humbly and with all of our hearts. Come and go with us."

PART 16

THE GREATER SIN

"Then saith Pilate unto him, Speakest thou not unto me? Knowest thou not that I have power to crucify thee, and have power to release thee? Jesus answered, Thou couldest have no power at all against me, except it were given thee from above: therefore he that delivered me unto thee hath <u>the greater sin</u>." (John 19:10-11)

THOSE CLOSEST TO JESUS

Why has the Church in America been unable to stop the downward spiral of society? Why is she seemingly powerless to stem the tide of evil which has ultimately become a tsunami of wickedness? How is this possible with a Church so well trained, so well equipped, so high tech, so promoted, so visible, so wealthy and so accepted?

In response, consider this; the word "Church" has been widely misused. As a matter of fact; it has been recklessly misused to identify a religious people, a religious place and a religious procedure. I use the word 'recklessly' because of its ultimate contribution rather than deterrent to the decline of our nation.

The logic of what I am saying can only be seen when the perspective is correct. The Storm which has taken control of this nation and is powerfully driving it is not chance nor is it coincidence. It is God Himself. The actions of certain people must be seen from God's perspective. It is then and only then that we will begin to understand God's response and how it is effecting our lives today and how we must prepare for tomorrow.

In this section I will endeavor to describe a religious people or population who has contributed to this national decline. It would be easy to refer to them as the Church, however, to do so would undermine the very truth I am trying to convey. Therefore we will refer to them as, "those closest to Jesus".

JUDAS ISCARIOT

I cannot imagine a greater criminal than Pontius Pilate the sixth procurator of Judah and Samaria. He was the one who ordered the crucifixion of Jesus Christ. He himself knew within his heart that Jesus did not deserve this horrible fate yet despite of his solid belief, he gave the order to execute Christ. Pilate's heart was hideous and his execution was heinous and yet Jesus points out an even greater sin than his. Jesus declares to Pilate that the power he wields is not his own; that it is given to him from above. At the same time, Jesus is revealing the greater crime which is committed by someone who has done it completely of his own volition, "…he that delivered me unto thee…"

There are many who were involved in this criminal act against our Lord, aiding and abetting to his murder. The "greater sin", however, must be attributed to the one who was the closest to Jesus among all of those involved with the Lords suffering. His was a crime of access and feigned intimacy. Indeed it had to be a betrayal of camaraderie, and trust. None of the others involved even vaguely fit this description. This individual can be none other than Judas Iscariot.

ONE OF TWELVE

In Matthew 10:2 we are introduced to Judas Iscariot as being one of the twelve disciples of Jesus. It's not long after that when he is described first in John 6:70-71 as being a devil and secondly in John 12:4-6 as being a thief. Being a devil sets him in direct opposition to the authority of God and as a thief one who would stealthfully take from God what does not belong to him.

The character and motivation of the devil was clearly seen in the words and actions of Judas Iscariot.. He soon realized the huge potential in the ministry of Jesus and the benefit it represented to him. Jesus became a means rather than and end to the desires of Judas. Positioned near Jesus meant power which would ultimately produce the prosperity that a thief like Judas Iscariot could have only dreamed of.

Judas was indeed positioned near Jesus but it was no indication of relationship much less intimacy with the Lord Jesus. Jesus quoted Psalm 41:9 as a fulfillment of prophecy in relation to himself and Judas Iscariot. In it Judas is called, "mine own familiar friend" (defined: man of my peace) a man who depended upon the Lord. In the end we see that Iscariots dependency was not based upon his love for Jesus but instead his own lust and greed. His life was never lived in response to who Jesus was but rather how Jesus might enrich his life.

WE FAILED TO SEE

This is exactly what we have failed to see through our modern religious eyes. That closeness is not a guarantee of love for Jesus nor is it an assurance of oneness with Him. Jesus is a discerner of these things. Any consistent approach to him without these virtues will ultimately become a source of pain and be seen as betrayal.

What then motivates the people's continual approach to Jesus? They are the things that motivated Judas Iscariot. They are the things promoted continually by "those closest to Jesus" and it is for them that people return. They are; position, power and prosperity. It is within this context that true salvation is taken for granted. It is essentially America's religious attempt to rise above the God

Storm, transcending the discontentment of God for our sins, in order to maintain and perpetuate the American dream. If not for all Americans, at least for those who go to church, get close to Jesus, and hear this message; "position, power and prosperity". This is the very reason sin is not preached. Accountability is not the pursuit! Don't you see? We mustn't betray "those closest to Jesus" even if it means betraying Jesus in the process.

WHY DO YOU THINK?

In John 13:2, Satan puts in the heart of Judas Iscariot to betray Jesus and then in Matthew 26:14, Judas bargains the betrayal of Jesus Christ. Why do you think Satan was able to put the betrayal of Jesus in the heart of Judas? It's because Jesus did not occupy Iscariot's heart. Jesus did not reign there. His own lusts and desires did. Judas did not love the King; he loved the throne and all it represented. Remember, Jesus was not the end for Judas; he was simply the means. Therefore the Lord's feelings had nothing to do with the deal. Like the thirty pieces of silver, the emotions of Jesus were only a minute detail. Iscariots aspirations were much greater. Of course he would rationalize his decisions along the way. That's what "those closest to Jesus' always do.

THE KISS

Let's see how this whole scenario unfolds in scripture and how it relates to our current situation. We find Jesus and his disciples reclined at the final Passover meal. According to custom, John (the disciple whom Jesus loved) being the youngest would be seated to the Lord's right. Judas Iscariot would probably be seated to the Lord's left considering he held the bag. He was probably considered the Lord's trusted one.

(John 13:21-30) "When Jesus had thus said, he was troubled in spirit, and testified and said, Verily, verily, I say unto you, that one of you shall betray me. Then the disciples looked one on another, doubting of whom he spake. Now there was leaning on Jesus' bosom one of his disciples, whom Jesus loved. Simon Peter therefore beckoned to him, that he should ask who it should be of whom he spake. He then lying on Jesus' breast saith unto him, Lord, who is it?

Jesus answered, He it is, to whom I shall give a sop, when I have dipped it. And when he had dipped the sop, he gave it to Judas Iscariot, the son of Simon. And after the sop Satan entered into him. Then said Jesus unto him, That thou doest do quickly. Now no man at the table knew for what intent he spake this unto him. For some of them thought, because Judas had the bag, that Jesus had said unto him; buy those things that we have need of against the feast; or, that he should give something to the poor. He then having received the sop went immediately out: and it was night."

TROUBLED IN SPIRIT

Here we see the agitation in our Savior. The time has come to reveal that one of his disciples will betray him. After years of being "one closest to Jesus" all Judas has to offer is ingratitude and treachery. And to such a degree that Jesus is troubled in spirit.

The ignorant betrayal of any and all human life is a betrayal of Jesus. How much more the betrayal of innocent human life by the most Bible based, Bible educated and Bible blessed nation in the history of the world! This deeply agitates the Lord Jesus in spirit. This is the source of The God Storm. So far from God, most are unaware of the agitation created in his heart because of our gross insensitivity toward his concerns.

THE BETRAYER REVEALED

Immediately the others want to know who this betrayer is! While all of this is taking place, we find John the beloved where he usually is, leaning upon the bosom of Jesus. His primary pursuit is of the heart of Jesus and he daily lays his own love upon it. This is a picture of the prophetic which hears the heart of God in all matters and concerns and it is through John that the inquiry is made. Deep love for Jesus will produce a laser like focus upon Him through which the power of God's Spirit flows, engaging every Spiritual gift and empowering God's people to be the voice and touch of God in this desperate hour. It's no wonder that John the beloved was used to write the Book of Revelation.

Jesus hands to Judas Iscariot the sop of bread indicating to the others who the betrayer is. Using this symbolism Jesus is saying not just to Judas but to all mankind who have or will ultimately betray him," I have put you before myself and have provided abundantly both for now and forever; and this is what you do to me in return?

JUDAS AND THE DEVIL

It is astonishing to find that in such an exclusive setting, so filled with divine purpose and the power of God, that the devil would not only be near by but would actually have full access to "one closest to Jesus". Without fear of Jesus; with out resistance from the betraying disciple and without reservation; the devil enters into Judas Iscariot.

If we were to suddenly discern the demonic activity within all Bible based congregations and organizations; we would be amazed! We would be stunned by the percentage of those not just greatly influenced by the demonic but totally available to it. When Jesus said to Judas,"…what thou doest do quickly", Judas had no idea that the devil had entered into him nor did he know that he would be known as history's most infamous traitor of all nor did he know that in a matter of hours; he would be hanging himself. Judas had a plan and now had permission from Jesus to complete it. He was completely oblivious to the consequence of his choice. It is the same for all who choose others things rather than Jesus, especially when they pursue them in His name.

Judas went about in an effort to manipulate the future of Jesus Christ for what was obviously his own benefit. It was a purposeful betrayal. This is where things become so touchy and incredibly dangerous. How much of our prayer is merely an effort to manipulate, perhaps the circumstances, perhaps other people, perhaps even Jesus (The Word of God made flesh).

Betrayal within the spiritual atmosphere of the Lukewarm is almost impossible to detect. It was then and there. and it remains here and now…"the greater sin". Even now the other disciples assume that Judas is dispatched to do good. In the same room, reclined at same table and yet they have no knowledge of the great betrayal that has just begun to take place. What the disciples didn't know about was the entirely "other life and character" of Judas apart from Jesus and the small group.

(Matt 26:45-49) "Then cometh he to his disciples and saith unto them, Sleep on now, and take your rest: behold, the hour is at hand,

and the son of man is betrayed unto the hands of sinners. Rise, let us be going; behold, he is at hand that doth betray me. And while he yet spake, lo, Judas, one of the twelve, came, and with him a great multitude with swords and staves, from the chief priests and elders of the people. Now he that betrayed him gave them a sign, saying, Whomsoever I shall kiss that same is he: hold him fast. And forthwith he came to Jesus and said, Hail, master; and kissed him." (Luke 22:48) "But Jesus said unto him, Judas, Betrayest thou the Son of man with a kiss?"

PRAYING OR BETRAYING

This is Gethsemane; the garden where the Lord often retired to for prayer. He has just completed the most important and difficult prayer of his earthly life to this point. Suddenly a great multitude of armed men rush into the garden of prayer led by Judas Iscariot. These men have been dispatched by the religious leaders of the day.

Judas had said to these soldiers that whom ever he kissed would be Jesus, the man they were looking for. Having said that, Judas walked directly up to the Lord, saluted him and kissed him. Once again, we see the amazing freedom and access that Judas had with Jesus. But we already know what kind of person Judas was. Furthermore, do you remember who had possessed his life? Wow! A man full of the devil and completely possessed by him has just kissed the face of the Son of God.

A kiss represents great honor and high praise but that's not what Judas is offering. His motive is not for the glory of Jesus. He's a thief! His is not a life that honors Jesus. His is not a heart that can offer true praise to the King. Oh he can get close to the Lord; and he can kiss the Lord. In the end, however, he is accomplishing two things. First he is only identifying him and secondly he is giving the devil access to Jesus through his own hypocrisy. Did you say, "No hypocrite can worship Jesus closely?" Judas did and…he…hath the greater sin"

OUR GENERATION

I believe that our generation has produced the greatest and most wonderful praise and worship the world has ever heard and experienced. It has caused my own heart to soar many times. Extraordinary worship leaders, singers that sing like angels and musicians that play as anointed minstrels from heaven all the while leading the people before the Lord…as they sway in one accord, like golden wheat.

Could ours be history's greatest kiss? Or could it be the greatest betrayal that any nation has ever placed on the face of Jesus Christ?

IT ALL DEPENDS UPON THIS:

(II Chronicles 7:14) "If my people which are called by my name, shall humble themselves and pray, and seek my face and turn from their wicked ways; then will I hear from heaven, and will forgive their sin, and will heal their land."

REACH OUT

The Bible tells us that Judas found no place of repentance and in absolute despair went out and hanged himself. Judas made a fatal mistake when he returned to the same religious system in search of repentance when they had not only solicited his betrayal of Jesus but had financially promoted it also.

No, we cannot return to the muddied waters of religion and expect the living waters of Christ. We must go directly to God through Jesus Christ our Savior and we must go quickly.

Start with your family. Invite others. Be open and sincere. Don't worry about what others will say. Strongly repent! Say to God, "Lord, what would you have me to do". Reach out to God in this raging storm and <u>He will save you</u>.

PART 18

AN UNSUSTAINABLE DEFENSE

21 And Rehoboam the son of Solomon reigned in Judah. Rehoboam was forty and one years old when he began to reign, and he reigned seventeen years in Jerusalem, the city which the LORD did choose out of all the tribes of Israel, to put his name there. And his mother's name was Naamah an Ammonitess.

22 And Judah did evil in the sight of the LORD, and they provoked him to jealousy with their sins which they had committed, above all that their fathers had done.

23 For they also built them high places, and images, and groves, on every high hill, and under every green tree.

24 And there were also sodomites in the land: and they did according to all the abominations of the nations which the LORD cast out before the children of Israel.

25 And it came to pass in the fifth year of king Rehoboam, that Shishak king of Egypt came up against Jerusalem:

26 And he took away the treasures of the house of the LORD, and the treasures of the king's house; he even took away all: and he took away all the shields of gold which Solomon had made.

27 And king Rehoboam made in their stead brasen shields, and committed them unto the hands of the chief of the guard, which kept the door of the king's house.

1 Kings 14:21-27 (KJV)

A NEW ERA

With this postscript chapter, I close this work. Time will prove the prophetic precision of it and ultimately (I hope) will prove to be as persuasive. We must be convinced that this is not just a season of unfortunate occurrences but a whole new era, from beginning to end the final purging and restoring of this great country. The sooner we embrace the truth of what is happening from God's perspective, the better. Early surrender to Biblical Truth during this God Storm will bring a much quicker end to its raging.

I assure you, this concept of 'New Era' is neither a whim nor the product of human imagination. The Lord has solidified its reality in me through an ever increasing number of incidents which could not have possibly happened coincidently. Past accuracies have contributed mightily also.

God will be glorified in this work. To Him be glory forever and ever. A new era has begun. The role of God has changed. Read carefully these final paragraphs. Amen .

IT'S BEGUN

Rehoboam was just one more step in the succession of moral failure among the leaders of God's people. The sin that was in the reign of Soloman, his father, continued and increased during his watch. The Bible clearly states that the sins of the people provoked God to an intense jealousy. Their sins had exceeded the sins of all the generations before them. They had become darker and more evil than ever before.

They chose to replace the True God with images, the creations of their own hands, devoting their worship to them almost exclusively. These counterfeit gods where placed everywhere. In other words, they were given priority in every aspect of their lives until the evil and sensual worship of them became a part of everyday life. Idolatry had become a lifestyle normal to the people. What was not obvious to them was the pain they were inflicting upon the heart of God. No other nation had experienced such pomp and privilege and all a product of the favor of God and though they had forgotten it, The Lord had not.

America so mirrors the image of this backslidden nation, it is astonishing even shocking. How are these similarities significant? Overwhelmingly so, because God does not change, he is responding to this nation the same way.

Then the Word of God briefly mentions a sin which had also become normal with the society. There were those who were practicing sodomy. To God, this was an indicator stating that the people had sunk to the depths of depravity. In fact, God had destroyed nations before them who practiced this very thing normally and regularly. In their debauched religions, this was an acceptable practice. Isn't it amazing, how that most of the most influential in our country consider sodomy (routinely referred to as something else) an indicator of our society reaching new heights of understanding and brilliance while God at the same time sees it as a ripened condition for destruction. Who do you suppose will win this debate? Watch and see.

FROM GOLD TO BRASS

In the fifth year of Rehoboam, Shishak the king of Egypt came up against Jerusalem. Shishak entered the once impenetrable city with ease and having great success in it took with him the huge treasures which King Solomon had amassed during his reign. Apparently Shishak accomplished all this with little or no opposition from Rehoboam! Many believe Rehoboam freely surrendered all this to the Egyptian king. Sin weakens all people without exception.

Then the Word of God continues, mentioning two more powerful details about the conquest of Shishak the Egyptian king. Before leaving, Shishak took also the shields of gold which Solomon had made. Later, being much impoverished by the conquest of Shishak, Rehoboam formed new shields but instead of Gold makes them of brass.

Gold represents the divine nature of God! Solomon's decision to make shields of gold was his powerful and accurate declaration that God had been the defender of Israel and the conqueror of their enemies. The golden shields declared that it was God who had prevailed on behalf of Israel and had provided for them every military victory. The fact that Shishak was easily able to take the shields of gold indicated that God's role as defender of Israel had changed.

With the Gold gone, Rehoboam made new shields of brass to replace the golden shields. In doing so the new role of God is revealed. Brass represents the judgment of God. Rather than the divinity of God alone, it represents the divine severity of God against sin especially in a purging and correcting manner towards those who have been students and recipients of God's law.

Rehoboam now holds the shield of brass. It simply means that Rehoboam has made God his enemy by refusing to serve and honor him through surrender and obedience. From now on Rehoboam will be forced to defend himself against the powerful judgments of God; a battle he cannot possibly win! Shishak represents impoverishment, a consequence of rampant sin; and against it, Rehoboam had no defense.

SUSTAINABILITY

We hear the word all the time. It has become a popular theme globally and now also in the U.S... It is the focus of summits and conferences worldwide. *Oddly enough, however, it seems to have become a rallying point for all anti-Christian, anti-Jew, and anti Bible nations of the world.

America, having crossed the line of God's favor, has in essence changed the role of God just as Rehoboam did. Refusing to surrender to the written will of God, America has made God her enemy rather than her defender as He has historically been. Consequently, America is found defending herself against all the difficult measures God is using to awaken her and to bring her to her knees in repentance. America has lost the shields of gold and replaced them with shields of brass.

Thus on multiple fronts this nation wars against the judgments of God: dwindling water supplies, dwindling food supplies, insect born diseases, pandemics, violence, super storms, increasing poverty, increasing social upheaval, cold irrational robotic violence, epidemic suicide, increased seismic activity and the lists goes on and on.

The perception of this wicked generation of intellectuals is clear. They conclude that most of our social and environmental practices have created unsustainability in necessary resources and must be changed. The changes advocated, however, are in effect an effort to maintain a good defense (a deterrent if you would) against God's correcting efforts. The proposal is to sustain the benefits of God's favor in the midst of His fiery disapproval!

WE CAN! WE WILL!

"We must create renewable and sustainable resources for ourselves. We must renew our planet and its environment in order to sustain its climactic health by reducing fever which will restore balance ending droughts and violent weather. We must create a sustainable social peace. We will revamp social structure in order to control its overall numbers, it's disparity of class, and it's extremes in behavior. We can control these things and we will control them in order to maintain our current progressive and enlightened advancements," they boldly exclaim.

As time goes by, however, these bold claims will wither as even the staunchest and most resourceful opponents of The Bible will weakly surrender, just as Rehoboam did before king Shishak without the slightest whimper of warring intent.

Although we have been the most creative, inventive, resourceful and determined nation in the history of the world, no defense against God's powerful call to repentance will succeed. It is:

AN UNSUSTAINABLE DEFENSE

7 But the heavens and the earth, which are now, by the same word are kept in store, reserved unto fire against the day of judgment and perdition of ungodly men.

8 But, beloved, be not ignorant of this one thing, that one day is with the Lord as a thousand years, and a thousand years as one day.

9 The Lord is not slack concerning his promise, as some men count slackness; but is longsuffering to us-ward, not willing that any should perish, but that all should come to repentance.

2 Peter 3:7-9 (KJV)

PAINFUL DIMINISHING

America, like Rehoboam's Jerusalem, has known incredible prosperity. And like that great society, diminishing wealth will be painful for ours. The tendency will be to blame one another. Desperation will develop and find its expression through violence and thievery. The better choice will be to seek God now. His desire is to restore us not to ruin us.

During this process, He will be acutely aware of those who have chosen His way and have surrendered to Him.

If you call out to Jesus Christ, He will find you. He will save you. And He will keep you. Amen.

13 For whosoever shall call upon the name of the Lord shall be saved.

Romans 10:13 (KJV)